An Invitation to Openness

Poems for Individuals and Communities
Seeking the Sacred in the Present Moment

Sue Sutherland-Hanson, MAT, M.Div.
and
Kimberly Beyer-Nelson, MA

Cover by Kathy Haug
http://ferncreekassociates.com/

Artwork by Mariah Leigh Ordonez
https://sites.google.com/site/mariahleigho/

ISBN-10: 1502467453
ISBN-13: 978-1502467454

Other Titles by Kimberly Beyer-Nelson

A Little Book of Wholeness and Prayer: An Eight Week Meditation Guide

At Matthew's Knee: A Poetic Commentary on the Gospel of Matthew
Vol. 1

Yeshua's Yoga:
The Non-Dual Consciousness Teachings of the Gospel of Thomas

Acknowledgements

Thank you, Abba, for the constant reminder: *Inana urha shrara wa hayye.* I hope I have written out of the kind of awareness that you constantly grace us with each day.

Kim Beyer-Nelson

I want to thank Kim for sharing her "can-do" expertise and energy, my daughter for sharing her artwork for the cover, my husband, who gardens the Eden in which I write, and the Intimate-Divine from whom I felt encouragement.

Sue Sutherland-Hanson

Contents

Introduction

My role in society, or any artist or poet's role, is to try and express what we all feel. Not to tell people how to feel. Not as a preacher, not as a leader, but as a reflection of us all.

John Lennon

Sue's Musings:

The idea for this body of poems started in the tiny bookstore of the Saint Placid Priory, a Benedictine Monastery near Olympia, Washington. Kim pulled a devotional off the shelf, called *Fragments of My Ancient Name*, edited by Sister Joyce Rupp. Having had the privilege of hearing this wise nun in person, and knowing both Kim and I adore Rilke's poetry from which came the book title, we knew that between the two of us, one of us had to buy this book written in response to different names of God.

Kim thought we might like to respond to these names with our own poems via email as a sort of on-line poetry project. The idea of encouraging poetry as a commitment to write and share on a regular basis took hold. I could not have imagined the good and many petals that would unfurl into this flower.

At first, we dutifully took on the names from Rupp's book like the Crucified, Forgiver, Redeemer, but soon we realized that these titles did not reflect the colors of the landscape in our journey. I do not regret our poems with these traditional names because I liked how writing in response to them cultivated a fresh understanding. We decided to draw from a wider source like the Muslim's ninety-nine names of Allah, Eastern concepts of the Sacred, and any other name that attracted our poem-searching eyes.

While both of us identify as Christians, with Kim as a comparative religionist and me as a life-long enthusiast of cultures, expanding the names felt natural, becoming a lovely way to grow our connection to peoples of other faith traditions.

Looking over the poems as a collection, I realize that several of them do not explicitly include any name of God. They seem rather to tell a story, show a glimpse, suggest a feature of the Divine. At first I worried that this strayed from our intention, but I abandon that concern in light of respect for the un-nameable quality of God. The Jews showed their respect for this feature of the Divine by referring to God with the acronym, YAHWEY. I suspect they knew that naming God can tempt us to the folly of trying to confine the boundless. Our poems without a specific name of God bow to that broadness of the Divine.

We send this book out into the world as hopeful as a gardener flinging seed to the wind. In fact, I picture you, the reader, able to smell our hope like a seasoning rubbed on each page. We desire this collection of poems to provide companionship to individuals traveling through joyful seasons of rest and consolation as well as challenging seasons of dark night depression, confusing paradox, or convicting moments requiring conversion.

We envision faith communities using this work in weekly services, various ceremonies, or as opening/closing texts for classes. We also hope this book sparks enthusiasm for creating in community by the example of our process. So often the vexed writer, holed up alone, dominates our image of creative process, but for many of us, we need and enjoy creating *with* each other. Doing so with our preferred art-forms can create a context for joyful community. Seeing our poems named KBN for Kimberly Beyer-Nelson or SSH for Sue Sutherland-Hanson should remind readers how communal this writing experiment was. Don't we all desire meaningful ways to connect? This book exemplifies a fun and creative way to be together in an isolating culture.

While we want this book to spark interest in writing with others in faith communities or writing groups, I want to acknowledge at the same time, the solitude of the deep and fertile well from which the bucket of spiritual writing draws. My spiritual mentor encourages my poetry and writing as she knows it provides a language of praise, confession, and chest-beating desire.

It is hard to write from that depth and not feel self-conscious as we cast about for an authentic voice. I cheer spiritual writers for their attempt to put words to what echoes from our depths because without this effort, how will we companion readers and for that matter, ourselves?

An unexpected support for writing into our authentic voice emerged with this project. Our exchange provided an instant and trusted reader for the other. This quieted the worry about who was going to read, reject, or react to our work. The safety of our friendship helped quell my fearful ego-driven critic who too often shouts over the quiet voice from my depth that whispers important things to hear. In our spiritual friendship, we could write what was real and at the same time enjoy a poetic chat like one might with a neighbor over a cup of coffee.

As well as listening to her poetic voice, Kim soon heard a clear directive to dedicate the first year's proceeds of this book to some arena of social justice, and I readily agreed. We both shared experiences in seminary where we felt very different from those with the zeal of activists; frankly it was easy to feel insufficient in an essential vein of spiritual presence in a hurting world, but we did not have the traditional edge of the activist in our makeup.

We soon realized that this act of donating and raising awareness was a way to employ a different kind of energy for social justice, one that includes communal arts and contemplative centering. Tying this example of justice-work to these poems raises a new set of hopes for the influence of this book.

Discussing which social-justice need to direct our proceeds provided a poignant experience of perspective and purpose. We felt rich beyond our means before the book was even published. And the resulting choice? The health of the earth and her oceans.

I came home from a Fisher Poet's Gathering with a heart broken and on fire for the ocean's care. As a daughter of a commercial fisherman near the Pacific Ocean, I grew up enthralled by the mythical nature of salmon and the mighty presence of the world's waters. Through many years of educational presentations sponsored by the fishing industry during the annual Fisher Poet's Gathering in Astoria, Oregon, I learned how our oceans are in peril through acidification.

Ocean acidification relates to climate change in that the imbalance of acids is caused by fossil fuel pollution sifting down from the atmosphere. The acidified water interferes with the development of exoskeletons of the tiny sea creatures at the bottom of the food chain. Whales to sea lions to salmon to octopi all teeter on the brink of destruction with the impending obliteration of their food source.

Normally this kind of information shoots me to despondent in a nano-second. In fact, I had suffered from years of paralysis with this information until I heard Kathleen Dean Moore, a writer, naturalist, and philosophy professor from the University of Oregon give a talk at the 2014 Fisher Poet's Gathering.

I attended Kathleen's slide-show presentation that focused on our moral obligation to care for creation. She filled her presentation with gorgeous slides, inspiring poetry, convincing facts, challenge, *and* hope, but only *if* we act in the slim window of time which remains. She sold me on the concept that this is indeed a social justice issue when we remember that justice is defined as acting on behalf of those powerless because they are without voice. And who are the voiceless in this unfolding drama? They are our children, future generations, and creation itself.

The moral imperative is to do what we can to repair our ways, so that we do not leave a legacy of destruction, a broken world for our children to inherit. Essentially it means educating ourselves in ways to move away from dependency on fossil fuels and pressuring politicians to support infrastructures that use alternative energy sources and to hold polluting corporations accountable.

I am a Christian who sees the mission of God, from Genesis to Jesus, as one of blessing people through shalom-wholeness in their relationships and communities. I find it interesting that our role for assisting in the repair of creation resonates by the same means: becoming communities that help each other live more locally, more simply, and more responsibly.

I've always loved how the Hebrew God of Justice challenged the wealthy and powerful of His people to care for the voiceless, the widows, and the orphans. If we don't feel rich as Americans, we are not seeing what we have. I cannot help but think of the earth as the widow, mothering us all. We risk leaving our children as orphans unable to be nourished by the earth on which our food sources depend if we do not act.

Kim became excited with me to use the proceeds of this book to raise awareness in how to care for creation including the oceans. We felt giddy at being able to weave together the arts, community, and justice. On several occasions, Kim and I revisited and soaked in the hospitality of the lively Benedictine nuns at Saint Placid Priory where each room is named for a mystic. There we used a room among many named for women saints like Saint Teresa and Saint Julian. I felt the presence and encouragement of these women.

I hope these poems attract your ear to a ringing truth that accepting the invitation to openness will result in the transformation of your eyes. May these poems help you see each moment's sacredness, deepening your understanding of the gift of your life and the privilege of living in the here and now.

Thoughts from Kim

A Tangible Act of Creativity and Compassion

As a child I wrote, "In the silence, I know the words will find me." It was the same way with music — those notes on a carefully lined paper made almost no sense to me, like putting a heavy screen between myself and the universe. I understood the theory of music notation, but what I could hear, even as a young child, didn't jive well with metronomes and time signatures. Words, like music, still seem to float all around me. If I observe a scene in nature, almost immediately I begin to tell myself the story I see there, assign words to branch and root, imagine who sat beneath a given tree and I create, in the space of a breath, their past, present and future thoughts and actions.

Needless to say, meditation has been a very good exercise for me to quiet that riot of associations and naming. (Yes, please grin with me here!) Centering Prayer has helped me to stay in a deep, silent place for long periods of time and to create enough space where I can, in my daily life, choose to fall into that dynamic dance of music and words or just simply *be*.

I live in my mind, mostly, writing science fiction, non-fiction and poetry, playing with fiber, teaching yoga and qigong. Occasionally, I teach comparative religion and spirituality-oriented adult education programs in the community or serve in the odd pulpit and I enjoy those times very much. But in my heart, I am a contemplative. I love simplicity, the press of trees, watching the birds at the feeder, turning the pages of a good book. My nervous system seems to need time to slow down, needs to focus on one thing at a time, and tease out the message that can be hidden in the smallest fungus and the wind that can sway a tree from its roots.

At the Priory in early 2013, a Benedictine monastery and retreat center in Lacey, Washington, I came across Joyce Rupp's book *Fragments of Your Ancient Name*. Each day, she suggested a different name for God, and I hooked up with my friend, Sue Sutherland-Hanson to try to write a poetic response to a name of God each day. I can remember her blanching, her soft voice telling me she didn't think she could do that *every* day. Turns out, I couldn't either. Between September of 2013 and well into 2014, I faced a whole series of hospitalizations and the fogginess of mind that goes with pain killers and the usual run of medical trauma. Still, by the end of that year, Sue and I had collected a sizeable mass of poems that ran the gamut from searching and dark night experiences to the exuberant play of community and joy. We ordered and indexed the poems while on retreat again at the Priory, ironically doing most of the work on a day that the community observed silence. What a bowl that place was, as we mixed and tasted the work of a year.

When faced with the challenges of our modern world — poverty, health care, the ecological issues, war, on and on, I am more often than not left wordless and exhausted before I begin. The incredible scope of such things, the immensity of the billions of lives of our world, these things are often enough to make the music grow silent and the words turn to inky mud-puddles in my mind. I am not called to hold signs, fight in the political or legal spheres, go door to door or even attend meetings about "social action". It's not that all of these arenas aren't necessary and good; it's just that they would be overwhelming to me. I would *feel* it too much, in a way that would be violent to my nature.

Such things are not my particular Way.

Sue and I had talked often about the frustration and helplessness we felt when bombarded with the many ills of our world. We felt keenly our contemplative natures, and how they seemed poor and flimsy in the face of issues needing action. And I think somewhere in that helplessness, a tiny seed of an idea took form. We would create a book from the poetry of watching this world and then gift the proceeds to an organization or individual that was able to do the big, relatively extroverted actions. We would also hold this chosen focus in our prayers and meditations, offering it/them spiritual as well as financial support. We would not let them drift from our consciousness. The person or organization would know they are *seen*, and by our seeing, others, too, could attend. We would choose to act locally so the personal and historical could brush fingertips with the larger epic movements of this part of our world.

It would be a small dance, a little jig, on a swirling and incredibly energetic dance floor, but it was a dance we could do, with joy and a sense of meaning. It would be our tangible act of creativity and compassion.

A word about words

Sue and I decided to read through our work and then create topical headings that best captured the intent of each poem. Those headings now include: Body, Perception, Present Moment, Praying, Discernment, Creativity, Cycles and Paradoxes, Mystery, Dark Night, Kenosis, Consolation, Rest, Relationship, Prophetic Voice, Trust, Joy. Words that spring from any religious tradition must be defined for a more general audience because of the history, circumstance and personalities that have added to or distorted their original meanings. But then again, perhaps *distort* is too harsh a word because the organic nature of language virtually guarantees such changes will occur.

We arranged the poems in a way that mirrors the way-stations along a spiritual path. I am more a labyrinth walker in my own spiritual journey — sometimes spiraling close the Center, other times flung out on the far curve of the pattern and thinking seriously about jumping out and going for a walk in the woods. Words help me create an inner pattern of meaning, my internal labyrinth if you will, and I know collectively they will eventually take me to the core of my faith.

As I look at the list, I'm quite conscious of three distinct movements- the first set runs from the Body to Creativity, the second set from Cycles and Paradoxes to Rest and the final set from Relationship to Joy. I'd like to look at these three meta-chapters if you will allow me to make up such words as I go!

From Body to Creativity

The dance of Body, Perception, Present Moment, Praying, Discernment and Creativity are the great tasks of any embodied being. So often, we try to define our spiritual selves without accepting the fact that we have arms and legs, little pot bellies and fuzzy armpits. That we get hungry and thirsty and sometimes feel downright sexy. All of these gifts have been given to us by God, and as we interact with the whole of our physical selves, we are also drawn into something incredibly profound: our senses themselves. These windows into the world act to bring us the images, smells, tastes, touch, and sounds of a cosmos far beyond our personal skin. Through them, we expand! From the joy of the body, we find the joy of the world, how it bumps up against us, delights and frightens and creates a holy awe within us.

In time, if we are lucky, we begin to make use of those senses without an overlay of emotions and conditioning and expectation and that is when we enter into the Present Moment. Here, all the senses are timeless, and we begin to acknowledge our own kinship with eternity. We begin to see we have only the NOW as the basis for our experiences, and it is in that NOW we have the room to make clear choices. But the glimpses of naked reality also can make us quail to our bones.

In those glances, we sometimes find ourselves brushing up against clear states of fear and giggles, withdraw and neediness, hyperactivity and torpor and the like--the reality of living, in other words. Both the pain and the ecstasy may then prompt us into prayer as a way to make meaning. We are relational creatures and in prayer we turn to words, our minds, emotions, intentions and attention and enter into the dance of the lover with the Beloved. We spiral into conversation with God and others at one end of the spectrum or the deep resting in the divine at the other, all of it prayer in all its diversity.

This can also become the bowl of discernment, when we hold and weigh experiences, knowledge, teachings and the call of our own heart centers that are continuous with God to enter into wisdom. We begin to understand the perils and gifts of free will and exercise the listening that is part of the body and yet also transcends it. We begin to trust that unscientific and relatively non-sensual states like intuition, compassion, gnosis and faith also have parts to play in creating a full life.

If we are earnest in such an embodied journey, very often we will want to share what we discover from these times — the meal well cooked, the painting, the music from our own hands, the poem. This dialogue with our world is critical; it draws us into the original movements of God, into the energy of Genesis that we are all heir to.

From Cycles and Paradoxes to Rest

The next movement of the spiritual journey is one of death. I know that sounds frightening and dark. But this is the death of the small self, as well as a call to be born again in a different frame of reference. We become aware of ourselves as constantly participating in cycles and paradoxes — we move through the hours of the day, the seasons of the year, the flow of our lives that constantly flow with energies of habit or the sweep of huge universal tides. We begin to see life not just as a line from point A to point B, but rather, a living spiral of sameness that is always new.

We also begin to be more comfortable with paradoxes — the falling tree is dead, yet its woody flesh lives again in the mushroom and the fern. The animal we eat is dead, yet it fuels this body and mind now, becoming part of us. Light can be a particle and a wave. We are finite creatures yet there is a part of us that recognizes we were never really born nor will we really ever die. Most importantly, we begin to see the world in the mode of woven relationships rather than this or that, black or white.

Something happens, then. We plunge right into the center of *God as God is*, which is formless, timeless, neither great joy nor great suffering, the vast I AM of the present, the steady state in the center of our own hearts. In India they call this Thusness or THAT. All our images, our ideas, our feelings are ripped away and we are emptied, which is the greatest grace God can grant us. Our discriminating minds flounder, and we find ourselves in the grip of the Dark Night of the Soul, as St. John of the Cross named it. Not a depression but a place ungrounded from all our pat answers and sure ways of knowing. We float without symbol or assurance or law and it feels that the darkness there will eat us whole. If we are lucky, that is exactly what will happen. We will be emptied of our little selves so that we can rise up like Paul and say, "Not I, but Christ lives in me." Or like the Buddha's "I am not an angel or God! I am Awake."

And then in that place of sovereignty, we begin to find a rest that is nothing special and everything wonderful. A rest that is everyday, engaged, mindful, non-combative and plain.

From Relationship to Joy

But the journey doesn't end in rest; it's simply that abiding energy that allows authentic actions in the world. Sue and I both tended to uncover the idea that from a base of rest, of apparent "mastery" of the spiritual path, we were again immersed in relationships, but with new "ears that could hear". Funny and painful, sorrow-filled or exuberant, our poems about relationship ring with the energy that "samsara is nirvana" and "nirvana is samsara". As we enter into the fullness of all temporal relationships we begin to manifest our kinship with God in and as Other and play out the energetic signature of "when two or more are gathered in my name, I am there amongst them."

Sometimes that energy leads us into a wholly different part of ourselves, the need to stand up as a prophet when we see either deep flaws in our world or startling glimpses of joy. We will often be very aware of those times when we wanted to edit this voice out, to silence what might be considered culturally inappropriate or frankly bitchy. The poems in this section are there to remind us that the prophet's voice is as much an authentic representation of the spirit filled life as joy or dark nights.

When we begin to allow this authenticity into our relationships with God and Others, when we stop fearing our ability to stand up, we find we have entered into a truly remarkable state called trust. Trust takes us beyond intellectual tap-dancing, and invites us into a space where the words of the spiritual joy start to fall apart. It is the central movement from belief to faith and lead inexorably to our final way-station, a state called joy.

In Joy we reaffirm the entire mess — spills and dog poop and politics and violence and grandchildren's grins and lover's embraces as well as the abiding presence of God. We open our arms wide and shout our YES! to the foundations of heaven and earth. For joy is the one inevitable thing for us all--our place of fecund growth and soft, secret abiding.

Ameyn-may this be the ground from which our new movements flow!

Body

Your whole body will be full of light.

Matthew 6:22

*Your body is the church
where nature asks to be reverenced.*

Marquis de Sad

Rain Maker

I am a child of the moss,
who does not scurry humped down,
rather looks up when it drizzles, mists,
even rains hard, who loves the sound
of forest dripping, who wraps in a low sky
of grey for comfort in quiet contemplation.

But even I cry *enough* come spring when
it seems my saturated bones lose their snap
in danger of dissolving into sod piles of soggy bone.
And who doesn't love the light when it rises clear and cold
then slowly warms the ground that steams its welcome up
as it riots down with quickened roots, twisting shoots,
readying for burrowing bugs waiting to move earth?

As for me, I plan to look both up and down by rolling
in the grass – my way of riot and welcome to the Sun Maker.

SSH

Seat of Heaven

Cup this flesh beneath your belly button,
the rounded center of your balance,
and lift your hands up, slowly,
broadening, widening
through gut and chest and shoulder
powerful and focused
then frame your head with open palms
feeling for the very center between
the hemispheres of your brain.
When you catch that place,
throw your hands up and out,
and grin or giggle.

Pull all that blue sky back to your mind,
sliding the hands down, down,
past hipbones,
past your knees,
brushing your feet,
all spacious, natural, light,
and release heaven to earth.

Now invite the ground back in,
directing it up with length and rootedness
until
heaven and earth mix in your belly,
stable below, spacious above,
the very
Seat of Heaven.

KBN

Earth and Mother
On my birthday – age 57

Mother of all mothers,
I am born into the body
of women who receive
seed and give birth,
nurse and nurture,
play and comfort,
hold in sleep, mystery
and death. Creator of all,
enlarge our laps, breasts
wombs, and hearts
that we may birth again,
grateful for earth as she,
hospitable, invites family
large and living to eat
by her garden
and find ourselves
in her good soil
as new shoots.

SSH

Breathing Wakan-Tanka

Cedar scented flute
lifts to my lips
as if gravity had fallen away,
and only my breath can draw it
close.
One finger always cradles a single
burnt hole, keeping it dark
but that frees the others;
light spills through now
and now
and now
allows the air to pass
no set pattern
no little black marks on a page
to contain life for this instrument.
Damp, warm,
my breath sinking into my finger joints
when I shut the various doorways again.
What is this sound but a
a place of flesh and wood meeting
and parting
hollow at the core of it all,
hallowed at the core of it all
as spirit washes through.

KBN

The Senses

Gates shall open for you;
there are no locks here.
The passage way between lies
narrow, focused,
the fossils in the stone path beneath your feet,
breathing still.
Can you swim as they do
in a salt sea of brilliant red?
And beyond, in the garden of paradise,
five evergreens sway, waiting.
Shall I name these five now?
Their roots like dendrites,
their branches like networks in your lungs?
This one, the eye,
capable of seeing everything in that first glance,
that one, the ear,
picking up pure vibration,
here one called touch,
feathering its needles in the wind,
over there,
the nose,
sniffing without regard both the sweet and the fire
and now,
this last,
tasting it all and finding it
good,
very good
indeed.

KBN

Quencher of Thirst

Laughter,
fingers wrapped around
ecologically conscious mugs,
I-phones turning off,
shrugging out of boots and coats,
water bottles with neon sipper caps
perch
next to yoga mats of every color—
grave-sized fields of rubber laid
over treated wood.

Play the CD,
old technology now
that can still skip and bump and jitter
when a mood hits it.

I love them, each one,
watch them as they stretch out
or chat, animated, with arms flung wide,
A confident people, shoulder to shoulder.
We move together,
tribe not crowd,
ancient patterns of simple, bare awareness.

And still, at the end,
with closed eyes,
arms outstretched over the cool floor,
I suggest a simple thing really:

Breathe in
"I am"
breathe out
"enough."

Always,
on their magic nubbed carpets
some will bring real tears
to offer to the Quencher of all thirst.

KBN

Backside

In yoga, the teacher reminds us to feel our backside.
We raise our bums and tuck our tails in pelvic tilt.

Her theme today is "remember, you have booty."
I smile as if she knows my secret: I see butts of all kinds.

Joining raunchy cowboys, I like horses with pretty heads
and big butts…and dancers and runners with gluts so big,

they can set a cup on their muscled shelf. I also sing
praises for my flatter, wider backside. For on these pads,

I meditate and moments rise when front and back
become one. Then I curl resting close to life

as if slung on the blade of a women's shoulder.
Curved in contour of the sling, my spine nestles

there in the palm of God or is it here,
in my heart, cupping the Divine's backside.

SSH

The Smell of God

Adam lay a hunk of clay, earthy and inert
until You breathed him into flesh, rising
and falling, smelling of tender warmth.

Did your breath smell sweet
as a new baby's whose body
quivers when the air of my face
brushes her skin and I sigh
suspecting her scent is yours?

Or did that first breath smell
of fresh hay chewed green as juice
of grass sprouts oozing over
muzzles and wafting scent of grass
over nostril-rims, elegant and soft?

So many creatures with your breath.

Other than a stink bug, I don't know
how the breath of an insect smells,
but I see how bubbles of spit hang
in clear clouds from bent stalks of hay.
I imagine a whale's mighty exhale
with the aroma of krill and sea.

I don't like the idea of dog breath
after seeing her eat manure, but
I grow tolerant absorbed
in the warmth of her eyes.
I don't like the smell of garlic
on a student's breath replacing
the papered air of my office,
but the perfection of his fingers
holding the pen and the hospitality

that he brings to receive my advice
gives peace round unwelcomed smell.

Quite in contrast, the aroma of coffee is
paradise, so why do I apologize for coffee breath
to the woman in choir? She has sense enough to say
"I love coffee" and I love her love of breath and coffee.

I rank as high as heaven the whiff
of melting mint on my lover's tongue.
I like to think that when I gasp my last breath,
I will inhale a mix of every perfect smell
I've ever known. Those I leave won't know
about my next first breath where I will sniff
a familiar scent of something good and forgotten.

SSH

Light

Sun stabs through my water glass,
defines a shifting world of
textures on wood,
little ridges of reflected flame
lapping into shadows.
The light blazes across my open book,
so brilliant I lose the words
in the pure, white glare
and pause,
tipping forward,
letting the sun play over the veins
and wrinkles in my hand,
pores wide open, casting micro-darkness
craters
like a moon face
hanging at the horizon.

KBN

The Cup

You poured yourself empty
showing the luminous curve
of your cup which would not pass.

Does this pouring teach me to drink
renunciation, spill my body,
pour out my mind, reject life?

Or do you, rebel of the heart,
raise your sloshing cup to thoughts
of beauty, sparkling emotions,

bodies that warm in a tub of touch?
Offer me this cup at the wedding
of the living, and I'm sure to be tipsy.

Teach me to drain each day's cup
and when I am served death, let me raise
my cup to all good lives and deaths like yours.

SSH

Shekinah

I have danced you on the yoga mat
thrilled to spreading
rootedness,
deep breathing expansiveness
dissipating
to the point
where mind became intuition
in the belly;
where I forget
all the names of God.

KBN

Liberator of the Soul

If the soul is some perfect part of me, a light,
an eternal rock, divine diamond connected,

reflected, reflecting, then what liberation
does my soul need? Freedom from my body?

How so when this body looks great
in lavender and red? I believe my soul loves color.

Freedom from life? Not likely- for this life,
full of joy, terror, beauty, and pain

ties its sacred self to the mast of my soul,
straight and true in the center of my aging ship.

Perhaps, this soul, shy and mysterious,
enters the light each time I bow to reality,

wrapped in the embrace of God.

SSH

Holy Spirit

Sounds like something I might yell
loudly
as twelve perfect chocolate chip cookies
tip off the tray and
free-fall
right into my hound's open mouth.
Or as I look out my window and see
my goat munching happily on my rose bush.
Flowers and all.

Again.

There is a food theme here,
and maybe that hints that I should
watch for spirit sneaking in around the edges
of the dinner table,
eyeing the plump pork chop and watermelon
and the pass-the-salt laughter.
Breathing isn't the only vehicle for the holy, after all,
just the lower-calorie one.

KBN

Radiant Rain

The cloud hangs black streaks into blue and yellow light
falling great drops of water, tinged with ice, onto the bay,
the beach, and cars, while walkers hurry for cover and look
for rainbows certain to please by fusing powdered colors
into an arched glow from the Cascade foothills to the ferry.

One passenger smiles at the radiance and thinks of her lover
and their inside joke, a *connection* if you will, to the lovers
in Song of Solomon, who spoke of his rain in their love-
making. Surely, she muses staring cross the bay, illumined
with bouncing rain, God's radiant rain falls from all forms
of love-making.

SSH

Perception

What the caterpillar calls the end,
the rest of the world calls the butterfly.

Lao Tsu

Giver of Rest

I leap out of the waters
calling for you: answer me
Creator of my silver strength!
    You gave me oceans of infinity
        to escape when pursued.
    Again be this gracious to me, and hear my
        Chinook prayer.
How long, shall my red flesh pock
    from shame of polluted waters?
 O How long will man honor words of commerce,
    that keep my young sickly?
Know that the Creator swirls the waters to gather
    the loyal for honor and delight;
She stirs the seas with her hands when I swim in search of her.
 When I fin in distress, I do not forget who I am;
    I ponder it in light and dark seas, and desire
    that I be true to my fresh and briney heritage.
I offer myself,
    in trust to decay and continuance.
Some fish die frowning in the murky silt.
  I ask, "Let the light of your moon-face shine
    on our scales."
I swim towards the river mouth glad in my bending body
    even more than when I fattened in the deep seas.
I will swim to my purpose in peace;
    for you alone, O Lord, make me
        rest in my royal calling.

SSH

Giver of Names

I say:
Robin,
Pacific Jay,
Red-Tailed Hawk,
Great Blue Heron,
Bald Eagle,
and he says:
bird.

I say:
Douglas Fir,
Maple,
Cedar.
Hawthorne,
Black Bamboo,
and he says:
tree.

Now the question is simple:
who saw Reality
more clearly?

KBN

Pilgrimage

I journey as hikers and pilgrims of old
have always labored, stepping along trails,
made difficult to pass buried under windfall
or made of shale, shifting under feet grabbing
with tilted ankle…the tired legs endure.

I think of gifts that surprise and strengthen
like light carrying sight of vistas to be absorbed
into our bodies, the earth with its resistance, coaxing
muscles to be strong, rock cairns placed by stone masons
who imagined future walkers in their steps. By their heaps
of good-will, muscles rest and tired backs straighten.

Gifts like snacks, sweet or savory shared on the path,
the sightings of critters, marmot, chipmunk, hawk,
who peek and let eyes catch a glimpse. Our bodies
seem to know we are connected to creation wild
in ancient places, fecund in our mysterious origin,
that is the One, who travels with us through each day,
through the living and dying of each season.

SSH

Radiant Rain God

Show me how to hold
a single raindrop on my fingertip,
balanced, crystalline,
its belly lifting skyward
middle-fingering gravity.

If I look closely,
an echo of me looks back,
distorted, water-colored,
then, with the barest shift,
it helps me to let it fall
with an exuberant (if tiny)
firework PLOP!
into my driveway's mud-puddle.

KBN

Hidden and Polishing

This deep self is the pearl of great worth,
the one the wise woman sells all to gain.

This self is the diamond on the black velvet
of the night sky where stars blaze, explode,

and dust the cosmos with sands of utter worth.
That grit enters the oyster that layers its luster.

Holy One, you are within me and I in you
in my truest place of darkness and light

better than any imaginably good news.

SSH

The Hidden One

Perhaps it is not that you are hidden,
but rather,
like a shy child at the edge of a party,
like the pup crowed up
trembling in the corner of the animal shelter,
like the new mother hen,
chasing around all the bits of fluff in her charge,
we let ourselves see too much,
feel too much,
try to control too much.
We judge and defend and race around
and I sense
even then,
all it takes is a moment's pause
to feel you: the one shadow in the world
that is warm and light.

KBN

The Ascension

My son, age eight gazes at his two samurai beetles,
the famed Kabutomushi in Japanese pet stores.
His eyes admire this bug version of a rhinoceros,
black and gleaming.

That night, we hear *click, clack, clack, click.* Tiptoeing down
the stairs, we see the source: exoskeletons caressing.

The next day, my son opens the cage to freshen the air,
and behold, one's plates slide open, and stubby wings
emerge, begin to whir, then spread blurring and whizzing
able to lift this armored lover up and away as we, amazed,
stand silent, stunned by the love-making and the leaving.

SSH

The Restorer

I love the days when
rain streams over my window,
flute music mainlined through headphones,
as I measure and consider
color, strength, texture,
even
the apple-pie smell of llama wool.

My mind is held in perfect tension,
my fingers warm with movement,
and yes, even when I have to stretch,
lengthening the muscles in my back,
I'm still immersed in the twist of the fiber, so
I forget to suffer with it.

KBN

My Rock and My Redeemer

Might a warring sailor think a redeeming rock to be the one
that juts barely above the waves and sinks the enemy's ship?
Might seven brothers, suffering from a spell that changes
them to swans each day, believe that tiny island, a rock just
big enough to hold them crowded, shivering each night but
buying enough time for their sister to sew nettle shirts, to be
a redeeming rock?

A mountain reaching from valley to thin-air heights, circles
gray stone walls round lupine fields, cut by streams curling
and clear, home to speckled trout holding place with flukes
swaying slow as butterflies drying wings at the edge of a cave
where bears ball into winter sleep by swales where marmots
pop to attention and whistle the arrival of summer hikers,
like me and my husband, who soak in the magic of this
mountain.

We pant scrambling over sharp scree that shifts and slides
under our boots seeking their place on top of this mountain.
We stand rejuvenated by views that swallow us with beauty
and adjust our sense of self, making us right. This rock
pushed thousands of feet into the sky now lifts and redeems
us, reward for our walking prayer.

SSH

The Subtle One

Delicate as the wire
making the see-through graph of the window screen,
fine as the pixels of the mountain photo,
ephemeral as a single fly's hairy leg
light as the peace candle's first orange-red flame,
haunting as three specks of cinnamon in chocolate,
ever-present as dust in the air,
cloying as the scent of drying lavender,
soft as the nap of Lamb's Ear beneath my touch,
mournful as the dove's first morning call,
I bow to you, Subtle One.

KBN

Immanent

At fourteen I sewed a suit of blue sail cloth, which I proudly
wore for one day until all the seams unraveled. "Oh My,"
said the teacher, rubbing her thin skinned chest, "this cloth
needs double hems. The devil's in the details."

While bridges stand or fall on calculation and seams hold with
exactness, I think of the poet's specifics, the ones who read last
night at the coffee shop, sharing fine points of life- a pool's
chlorine, red and white pinto beans, a Parisian bike with thick
handles, a marble, blue and smooth rolling down a path of
stone and grass into a dirt hole.

Renewed faith in details fills me with determination to praise
particulars like the bend in stems of daisies leaning over
hostas, the hydrangea heaping blew starlets over lambs ear,
the steady bird call, sounding like plans for the day's work,
the wetness in the air beading on bunches of black grass,
the lavender that lost its purple but not its perfume.

Bridge builders and seamstress must obey accuracy or fall
naked into seas while poets and mystics dance with the
divine, playing tunes to entice our noticing creation's details.

SSH

The Miracle Worker

These two words together,
Miracle and Worker,
imply an agency that intervenes,
that overwrites the functionality
of the system we *like* to name reality.

But what if a miracle is only
that which we could not see before,
a lifting of a veil so close to our nose
that it felt like skin, felt like a boundary
and we now know it only by its absence?

And worker? Well,
it is said all things must act, even God.
If the divine is without one name, surely
it is also without one action; all
work breathes out, even the unrecognized variety.

So how best to lift the veil?
How best to act with the Lord?
Listen, my friend, in the way
of those who have ears,
and with eyes that are ever new.

KBN

Present Moment

Realize deeply that the present moment is all that you ever have.
Make the Now, the primary focus of your life.

Eckhart Tolle

Invisible Reason

Break and shatter the sunlight on
long limb
and waving green,
swirl in the Stellar Jay's cry,
raucous before the autumn, daring
the rains to come.
This is fall's delight,
the tinge of all things a little manic,
squirrel hanging by one paw to grasp
an Italian plum,
sheep pressing the fence against their chests,
calling and stamping at the strange dog
raiding the compost pile.

I can play at meditative movement
but today,
I will be bursting,
insides as restless as waving grass,
the reason just as invisible.

KBN

Creator of the Shimmering Sound
(Neil Douglas-Klotz)

As a child, I used to perch on my bed
the buzz of mosquitoes just beyond the screen,
the wind, murmuring through the twin Jack pines,
the rumble of the jet overhead--
Indiana Air National Guard night training flights.
I would shut my eyes
trusting
I would hear beneath it all,
a single, pure note,
not quite a buzz,
less breathy than a whisper,
but more alive than a struck chime.
A felt sound,
that made my inner ear wobble
and my nostrils flare,
incredibly intimate and yet
and yet
the trees and bugs and jet pilots
were all upheld on that one
perfect note.

And then,
only then,
would I dare to pray.

KBN

The Serene One

Santosha,
Contentment.
Say it again,
low in your heart and mind.
and as you bow to your yoga mat,
as you run through why you are here,
for weight loss and stress reduction,
for bone health and flexibility,
for focus and strength,
Pause.
Consider.
What if your practice was simply
about
being right here,
palm to palm
and every asana in the world
perfect
before you even begin?

KBN

Cheating for Gratitude

She keeps a bowl of good words, and each day
she stirs the bowl with her finger to pick
the word for a day's reflection. Today, she stares
at *expectancy*, says it aloud, witnesses herself hearing
little resonance. Meanwhile, the coffee brews, apples stew,
the sun climbs behind the pointed firs, blue hydrangea hang
papery and glowing. She adds cream to the apple sauce and
her coffee that pleases like caramel. Coming to her senses,
she wonders what more she need expect and cheats (in a way)
stirring the bowl until she finds *gratitude*.

SSH

Lord of All Eagerness

Haven't you leaped up,
clapped your hands,
feet defying gravity
lifted by humor or creativity or love?
If God is stillness and being and holding,
God must also be the
wave on the beach,
the explosion on the sun's face,
the wild wind in the fir
the puppy chasing its tail,
everything whirling and restless
and Going Somewhere,
if only
so
we catch the perfect tulip,
bathed in a ray of light,
immovable,
timeless
now.

KBN

Green tea

Floats steam over my quiet keyboard,
smells like mossy rain-drenched sky,
and softens the crust in my eyelashes.

Today I will teach in water,
teach in a library with children,
walk a sodden racetrack with a friend,
dig a novel character out of a tight spot.

But just now,
only the faintest breath moves the fir boughs.
I can hear my teenager snore.
And I take courage with my first bitter-sweet sip.

KBN

Glorious One

A ribbon, a slash of sunshine
runs like the path of a spotlight
over my computer screen.
And all the words beneath it blur.
Glory is like that,
cutting through it all,
the runner-high, the caffeine spike.

We do clouds best here on the coast,
gray stillness woven with green,
so when the light strikes,
making the moss dance like fire,
we perk up for a moment,
smile into its brightness,
shy and intrigued as strangers meeting.

Ah, now the light has moved again.
I can see my words, refreshed,
my novel character dragged on through the night
by hands he does not know,
and I reach out to tap at white on black keys,
that he, too, might stumble into
a moment's glory.

KBN

Quencher of Thirst

I thirst for progress watching how my strokes move me
slowly through the pool measured by cork line and flags.
My fingers touch the wall and I reverse. Competing,
I take note of faster swimmers; my body slows, rebelling
at comparisons.

I practice in the pool to gain confidence in lakes where
progress won't be measured by lanes or swimmers.
I imagine the lake, where I must trust persistence and
my breath to mark progress, count my strokes, stay rhythmic,
insist I not panic in the expanse of water with no wall to tap
or swimmer to grasp.

Once in the lake, I glance at the distant shore to check
my course, find my progress imperceptible, feel the threat
of panic close, but then I look up and lose myself in the blue
expanse, so I forget I need be anywhere else.

SSH

Embodied

I stand at the lake's edge in a crowd of swimmers squeezed
into black wet suits ready to begin the race.

I am not competitive – I might come in last. Nor am I
concerned. My pay-off comes from a gift-giving body.

We eat and drink stories of past glory and failure the night
before. We savor the salmon and pasta that will fuel us.

Since body anchors the present when I am in the water, I
marvel at the buoyancy of it and the blue of the sky.

On shore again, we lie in the grass, relaxed, precious and rare
this way of being and together.

We share our highlights. Mine is how the crowd, their joy and
effort moved me to tears.

Physical, limited, and fragile, my body holds the mystery of
life's largeness. I long to befriend this body that holds
the presence and number of my days.

SSH

Praying

Prayer is where the action is.

John Wesley

The Enlightened One

I wrestle the divine for understanding,
at times panicked as a horse pulling back,
wild with fear and savage energy to escape
the rope that traps it. Once I watched
my mare nearly break her neck thrashing
pitifully against the chain that bound her,
but then mysteriously the whole post pulled
and she froze, quivering with sense to stop
though one end of the post hung swaying
from her chin. Quivering yet still, I could free her.
Like her, not knowing the origin of my panic,
I halt when something gives way and somehow
the need to stop arises. Now, when fear jolts me
into a bout of thrashing, I expect a coming calm,
the unhooking, the broken fences that lead me
to new fields.

SSH

Spirit of Putter

Scoot your butt to a wall
and slide your legs up it,
just like you're sitting there,
back on the floor, feet in the air,
gravity suddenly quite strange
and the view? wholly odd!

See how long before
you create a shopping list,
rerun an argument,
desire a chocolate ice cream sundae
with a cherry, no less.
Maybe you can feel the whole
cascade
the momentum of the mind,
rushing downhill
until
you really see
the flat place at last,
and really?
it's
not
so
scary.
Lord, give us this day
a spirit
of putter.

KBN

Agent of Blessing
Trust All Joy Theodore Roethke

Currents of people flow onto the boat as a few stragglers
move against the crowds disembarking. I look at their faces
for their story–are they going home from a night of work
or beginning their day? Meeting a lover in routine embrace
or in passion after absence? Facing a sadness or a joy?

The phrase, *agent of blessing* keeps rising like steam
on a summer day's tide flats. It's a bookish term,
which I'd dismiss but for its insistence, wave after wave
heaving upon the shore of my mind, traveling as from
a wake of an unseen but familiar ship. I decide to play
with the phrase, make a game: secret agent of blessing,
wherein I pray for those people going ashore as I see
their faces and crane my head to follow, then shoot
prayers aiming at them as prey. I imagine something
zinging their interior, wonder if they feel something,
some good surge of mystery.

What do I feel? I mumble inwardly as if repeating a question
just asked. Like my father tapping the barometer, I check
my gauges and observe current conditions. My spine
has stretched into the same tallness as after yoga; my chest
warms as it does when surprised by beauty, and I notice how
I relish the elasticity of my lungs filled with salt air. I breathe
with the same pleasure as eating dessert. Like Bond,
James Bond, I live the high life of a secret agent.

SSH

God of my Bitter Hours

My first theology class,
Jesus Christ Superstar,
Living room rock
That still rolls and thunders.

Third grade,
I sang Jesus' part,
"Take this cup away from me,"
and felt the first stirrings of
Compassion.

I still know the opera by heart,
even when bits of it
are foggy
in my mind.

KBN

Cowboy Spirit

I wrap in a blue shawl on my front porch,
where I want to make quiet rambling thoughts,
gather straggling senses that raise dust
with their wandering, having lost sight
of our desired destination of green fields.
These stragglers miss the warmth and rhythm
of moving together, swaying flank to flank.
Skinny thoughts nibble on dry shrubs.

I see now why I spur my focus yahooing,
galloping round the loners, urging them
to head in one direction Truth is that here

on my porch, I smell lavender rather than sage.
I hear birds rather than lowing, but I sit content
surveying interior plains thanks to cowboy moves
like slapping rope on chaps to round up stragglers
and move out as a calm herd walking.

SSH

Hallowing All My Acts

I used to believe
I could, intelligently,
Sift through data,
Follow research to its
Pristine source.
Trust the words of
Teachers, doctors, economists because
They could follow those trails
That were too complex for me to tread.

And I used to believe, when called to act,
I could trust my gut,
My empathy,
The whole language of body and eye,
So that words wouldn't matter as much.

But often, now, I find everything suspect.

The death of any naiveté
Is not so much a barren, logical end-place,
But the deeper hurt
Of knowing
How difficult it is to be
A wholly relational being
In relative reality.

Can Thou, then, hallow all our acts?

KBN

Silence

This week feels expansive as I celebrate
my retirement after thirty years of teaching.
I do not eat much; giddiness fills my stomach.
I seem to be floating in a hard helmet
of steaming thoughts spinning without start
or finish in a timeless space beyond the known.

Like the astronaut cut from the ship, I panic
and jerk fumbling for my placebo of busy-ness
to help dull the terror of vastness. After the parties,
but in my first week, a moment of calm shows me
I am not untethered, but free. Not in black space,
but on an ocean teaming with life. Curiosity makes
me hungry and brave so I lean over the bow
peering for food, rocking on tides that pull me
where they will – this time to the shore, where
I pull the skiff over the sands and reach for my catch.
My sustenance is silence.

SSH

Bough of Blessing

I stayed up with him all night;
watched him paint the walls slimy green,
his sides heaving
head hung low.

He watched me with his silvered eyes,
and cried out loud, like a child,
when he hurt too much.

It's hard to explain to a goat
that Rhodies are poison;
green means go, good, gobble
and all boughs are blessing, right?
Here, I'll squirt down more mylanta
and vegetable oil and
something for the pain.

This morning, he wanders around his paddock,
all cleaned out and deflated,
vaguely apologetic about his own
smell.

But still he eyes the smooth, wide leaves
and wild sprays of pink flowers
the place he is not allowed to go,
his jaw moving contemplatively,
still called by the green.

KBN

Servant on Maundy Thursday

My workshop writers, brave and open, scratch
their poems responding to the prompt, shoes and
death. Reading their just-written work aloud,
we cry at the images of little white shoes, empty,
size newborn, bronzed boots, honoring boys,
who stepped wrong, a mother's garden loafers,
left by the door. The very air sparkles with creativity
we gift each other when we are together.

Departing, we bend, collecting purses, mugs,
and notebooks before the talk turns to next-time.
Ah, I see it is Maundy Thursday, the day Jesus
commanded us to love as he loved and demonstrated
by washing his disciples feet. With boldness I am
possessed, and ask each writing friend if I can obey
Christ's commands in the same ancient way
and bless through their feet. Bemused, they agree.

Strange that I used the words, *obey and command*
for I left those words on a heap, topped by an image
of a broken, bully god. I kneel to bless my friends' feet,
Christian, Buddhist, Jewish, agnostic, pagan. We know
without speaking that we worship together offering
our sacred depth in the words at the altar of our hearing.

Their feet arch round in the cup of my palm. My grasp
loves as only hands can; their gaze, brief and infinite
touches like only eyes can. I keep my experience quiet,
do not tell what Jesus knew: to hold a foot like this,
is to touch God. I crawl atop my discarded word heap,
take back *obey* and *command* with my hands still buzzing.
Obeir first meant to pay attention and *command* to entrust.

SSH

Morning Star

I wake with the birds now,
their cries, brilliant,
nudging into my dreams
like wind chimes and
water over rocks.
Of course, it's only five A.M.--
plenty of time to simply stare
up into the pines catching
the very first light,
and when I am lucky,
the faintest morning star
to wish upon
as the night folds itself
into moss and
the hollows of seashells,
passing like a stranger,
weaving its way to bed
even as I begin to contemplate
wings and seeds and sky.

KBN

Gracious Creator

Lately, the verdant green, yellow, white, blue,
the bird song, rooster's crow, the brook, singing
on its way to the sea as it waters roots along the way,
the shhh of cedar fans and doves, the scent of dawn chill,
becoming perfume on warming Daphne, the brush of breeze-
all this makes me fine with the idea of dust to dust. Add water
and we are earth to earth. I only ask this: let me for all time
know I am in you as I know now and from time to time
in this body, in this way.

SSH

Servant of Others

I bow before I enter
the yoga studio, martial-arts style.

No, I know, it's not a dojo
or a church.
But still,
the space about to be filled,
dark now, and cold
breathes ghostly, with imaginary strips of rubber
barely cushioning the wooden floor,
sighs with the release of muscles
held so rigid in expectation and aggression
and fear.

And before I switch on the lights,
urging the colored bulbs to push back
against the mirrors,
and the weight rack,
hunkers,
shrugging darkly in its
vaguely medieval glare,
I ask a simple thing
to the silence there—
Lord, make me an instrument of thy peace.

And bow again, servant heart
hand-fasted with a warrior's mind.

KBN

Flute

Too many holes make a useless lattice of my flute.
Today three people forgot they ever met me,
yesterday- submissions rejected;
discouragement carves black holes,
that do not sing.

Attempting silence, I greet God
with a sticky sigh, wince at a text of praise,
the Psalmist shouting, *my heart sings*!
so I exhale my request: *Help my heart sing.*

Once a sparrow mightily filled her lungs,
threw her head back, opened her beak,
and twilled unabashed ecstasy.
I hear that song nearby
and decide it is today's teacher.

I throw my head back, open my mouth,
and copy that song nothing like
that sparrow's dervish of wild notes,
all of which makes me laugh.

A gust of air flies out with my "ha!"
mingling with the breath of God, making
music through me, now a perfect flute.

SSH

Source of All Being

Oneness.
Manyness.

One seed, nestled with others.
One root, branching out, fingers on a reaching hand.
One leaf, many strips of green, singing, windblown.
One tree, amid the forest, swaying.

Can you see both at once?

The scale and the fish,
the feather and the bird,
the tomato and the garden,
the rock on the beach?

Then you are a mystic, my friend,
and beginning to see
into the source of all being.

KBN

Becoming an Octopus

Through the practice of deep quiet,
I become an octopus.

Bones no longer resist, so now I tuck
and rest in rock crevices. Skeletons
of cherished thoughts soften, form
round wily wisdom of large mind.

I have more arms to embrace what I love
and break the backs of sharp toothed lies
that would eat me belly first. Tentacles anchor
in strong currents in this under-heaven world.

My sharp beak breaks hard shells of paradox.
I eat mystery in caves of solitude while eyes
of light, markets, and easy faith try to understand
mystery outside of depth. Outside of my element,
I have no shape, and the mind slaps formlessness
at the water's edge trying to tenderize and digest me.
And I will nourish them once, but in this way, they

cannot taste the beauty of my changing colors, peace
in my black ink, or the courage to brood until death.
As Christ of the deep, I let rise from my dying self,
translucent babies swimming, a thousand lights churning
tiny legs. In this darkness, I become a thousand floating suns.

SSH

My Help

Caught a bit of a caffeine high yesterday-
walked,
laundered
washed windows and dusted,
planted green things in dark soil,
cooked with cheese,
edited and visited on-line,
but
I don't recall how the sun really felt,
and there must have been the sound of spring birds.
I can't remember what
my son had discovered on his computer,
and I was told that I had missed the sheep
pronging over the meadow like lambs.

Lord be my help,
if only to give me a holy
brake.

KBN

Keeper of Memories

They tell the story of the little girl,
asking her newborn brother
to speak of the home he left
before they both forget. Of course,
he couldn't answer. We never can.
I think how great joys, tenderness,
beauty re-mind me, something familiar.
I recall that I used to speak mystery,
my original language.

Perhaps those brief eternities re-member
as we move again to whole.

Perhaps these moments are true prayers
when winds lift the veil and we dream
we see you, cradling us before we left.

SSH

The Compassionate One

Abba,
I have walked the desert of the intellect
for days now,
defining words
questioning senses,
laying the lines of unity
out in precise language.

Today, my stomach is rebelling,
nothing stays down,
not even something as dense
as tea.

Today,
I will just feel,
unpleasant as it might be,
and yet be thankful
for
the spaces of quiet
when the mind just rests
in your compassion.

KBN

Al-Qabid y Al-Basit
Constrictor and Expander

Do I want to know you *now?*
As if I could jump off a spiritual cliff
with a *yes.* Isn't it more like, you breathe me
and ask that I trust my lungs as the air
comes in, goes out, constricts, expands
the continents of tissue in my chest,
ebbing and flowing, here and here,
now and now. *Welcome* I try to say.
Flow I want to say, but your Spirit
 goes where it will, crashes like the ocean
against rock cliffs, exploding into foam.
And then you draw away, breathing tide.
And then, you are a quiet pool
by dark river rock where salmon rest,
tails swaying, gills expanding, constricting,
somehow breathing, dying, birthing.

SSH

My Salvation

Roll yourself over me
a healing salve,
not the fireworks of resurrection,
nor the stammering awe of the new-breathing dead,
just the breeze off the Sound today,
mountains snow-capped and wreathed with light.
Just this sun on my face,
filtered through the fingers of fir.
Just this tiny bud on the lilac,
soft beneath my thumb.
Guide me to a high place,
set my feed firm in the slippery mud,
And know I will tip my head up,
and receive.

KBN

Flute Player Krishna

Blue-skinned swirl,
you moved as breath,
each woman knowing
you danced only with her.

Teach me to yield like that,
to allow a holy air to blow through me,
my heart the backbend,
my mind, the expectant white-board.

Teach me to be compassionate like that,
so each pair of eyes becomes the entire universe,
so each hand on my elbow,
the very touch of God embracing God.

Teach me to dance like that,
touch and release,
lightness suffusing everything,
so I might flow with it all.

KBN

Discernment

Who would search for pearls must dive below.

John Dryden

Fortress

Twine, now, the thorny vine
blackberries not yet ripe,
leather girded hands and
sharp cutters to wear down the green wall,
while the goats work alongside,
gleefully eating what
snags at cuff and scores the skin.
Fortress or salad?
Perspective is all.

KBN

Rage

Have you eaten that cold rage,
hoping
for a little warmth between your ribs
and found instead
how it binds
your fists,
wrinkles the skin between your eyes,
lifts your shoulders to your ears?
And woe if you try to speak out of stomach full like that.
It is not enough to swallow the fury;
we must invite it to the table within
sit it down,
tip our head and listen
so it may settle into our bones
a more civilized beast
holding up the mirror to our face.

KBN

Life

Shake an egg a little against your ear,
slosh up against the shell
in your imagination.
Then look around you.
What egg whites cushion you
just now?
What pale barriers,
so formidable,
are actually permeable,
like a boiled egg dipped in beet juice,
just aching to let in all shades of
purplish red colors
to paint
your belly
with life?

KBN

Breath

My sweet friends,
be careful with your breath.

If the mind is filled with universes
and the smallest microbe,
can you doubt the force of all of that
lasering into speech?
One in-breath is still Alaha Ruha,
The Spirit;
with the out-breath that speech rides,
our smallness tags along
with the excesses our body no longer needs.
The out-breath is one of our kidneys,
really.

Even that shaky recognition about what is
in
and
out,
has started wars.
I like the startled surprise of the in-breath—
a prayer all its own.
The choice of the out-breath's message,
well...
that I must leave to your
loving
discernment.

KBN

Honesty and Tenderness

Three days in a row I pick the same angel cards despite
my efforts to avoid them: *Honesty, Wisdom, and Tenderness.*
I hear the voice of self-doubt, an old familiar charge
of insufficiency. The woman I am becoming responds.
I put on my big-girl panties, spiritually speaking, and sit
holding the question: *what am I to learn?*

The disciples ask Yeshua about fasting. They want to know,
is fasting what God wants? Did they scowl in confusion
at Yeshua's response, a real non-sequiteur: *stop lying and
doing what you hate.*

Funny that Yeshua so often asked people what they wanted
as part of their healing. Scholars call Yeshua, *Sophia,* meaning
Wisdom. How is it that so many link suppression with
wisdom when Yeshua calls wisdom to marry desire.
This is a marriage of love and we need honesty to share
what we want.

On the fourth day I question my words and hold them
in prayer:
Honesty? Show me what you got.
Wisdom? Sympathize, please.
*Tenderness? I need healing, rest, and strength for the hard work
of living and desiring.*

SSH

Naming and Knowing

Name an object,
and you think you know it.
Name a person,
the same happens.
Conflate object and person
and you'll reap misery a hundred fold times.
Pass on Mystery with words? — good luck.
The little mystery of communication
tangles on itself while
the greater Mystery
shakes such dust from its feet,
reaches out to help the neighbor,
drinks the wine and eats at your table.
And when you see the Mystery then,
just out of the corner of your eye
where words cannot quite reach,
then will you light up,
the next Big Bang already in motion.

KBN

Density

Still this morning,
clouds packaging tree tops like ornaments
the wind politely letting me breathe
across a blueberry leaf to set it trembling.
If there is an opposite to solar power, I am that,
radioactive in the mist
occasionally toxic, but
the trick is to see where the need is for the energy,
currents of loving, creating, listening,
and to keep sending it all out and out
instead of collapsing into density.
With no sun to compete with,
on days like this?
Well,
I am more aware of the inner glow
in us all.

KBN

The God Who Breaks Chains

Not everything that binds us is overtly dark and depressing. But one thing that many chains have in common is the idea of *must*. I must do better, try harder, be more than myself somehow. I must show my blue ribbon, my A grade, my high salary in order to be of worth. I must love everyone, be bright and cheerful every day. I must serve and support, nurture and balance the world around me. Must is really the word of exhaustion, a slave-maker. Try to say, "I am enough, just as I am." Do you believe it, in that place in your heart where you and God waltz?

KBN

Husks

The nuthatch perches on the squirrel-proof feeder
(the squirrels didn't read the blurb about it)
flinging seeds in a spray of glistening black and tan.
He pauses,
flips his tail at my study window,
and dives in again.
Presently, they come:
the spotted towhee and
the dark-eyed junco,
and a single dark-headed gross beak,
the ground feeders who vacuum up and take away
the kernel on the wing,
letting the husks separate and settle
into the mud.

KBN

Liberator God

There are things I could pray for:
freedom from self-guessing,
from imposing an image over my
own sense of who I am.
If I get started, I suppose,
the list could grow
endlessly.

I'll spare you that.

Instead, I would ask
for one simple thing:
dispel my ignorance.
hold up the mirror
kept in the most secret space,
that I might see You
looking back at Yourself,
laughing.

KBN

Creativity

There is an instinct for newness,
for renewal, for liberation of creative power.

Thomas Merton

Seeds of Enlightenment

Instant enlightenment never worked for me;
yeah, I could see
the cold water closing over my head
would make me scream "NOW"!
right out to the ends of my soaked hair.

But usually, enlightenment settles like
blown dandelion seeds on our skin,
tickles and departures,
leaving us to scratch a bit in wonder
and walk around
making up poems about it
afterwards.

KBN

Inspiring Spirit

Breathe in,
in-flate,
until your ribcage aches,
your heart leaps,
your chin lifts,
spine grows long.

Throw your arms out, fingers spread,
lift to your toes
and capture
that first raw explosion of creativity
that birthed matter
and suns
and you.

KBN

Lessons in Imagination

"Prayer is the supreme act of the creative imagination," Henry Corbin

Today, the lesson, the language, the teacher
is imagination, driving me bouncing and swerving
over mountain roads inside me, high and untraveled,
rutted and overgrown to the trail-head, where I,
on this interior trip, attempt silence, patience, hoping
to spot the illusive art of being, hoping it will show itself
and stay long enough to see clearly at this edge
of my wilderness. Waiting sets my imagination to weave
a tenuous bridge between intellect and senses.

Loop, pull, yank.
Waiting and imagination summon creation.
And then

my skin tells me something approaches, something divine,
someone shy that wants to be known, but like all wild things
fades before direct gaze.

Do I imagine laughter
at my disappointment,
my excitement, at this trick
into knowing?
My truest poem is voice and tongue of prayer,
the language of being that sings what I see
from that swaying bridge.

SSH

The Tomb-Opener

Take this book upon your lap;
no, I do not care if it
has stood the test of centuries,
nor do I worry about the bloodlines
of its authors.
It will have many faces, depending
on the light, on your years,
on how the wind feels right now,
spring-soft and pollen-swollen.
Open it at random;
play is the spirit of life,
and read what today speaks.
A million times, you could see
the same words,
watching until the paper itself grows
yellowed and fragile, the ink
smearing into something like
the secrets of neuron whispered to neuron.
Open the book, any book,
and grow larger on the breath
given form.

KBN

The Disturber

He fluffs himself,
preening,
the sun bright on his
red splashes of color,
dapper bib,
stripes meticulously combed
with his bill.

How to stand out here,
how to be heard,
where the ferry calls,
the cars hum
and even the children's
bright laughter and playful shouts
fill so much space?

Surely she waits for him.
If he can disturb her enough,
perhaps she will alight close by,
shy and impressed,
tipping her head to see him with both eyes.
He snuggles closer to the silver tubing.
Strange tree it is,
hot and spewing out smoke
when the island shivers in winter.
Dull reflections of himself startle him
but only for a moment.
Tentatively he taps
and OH! The sound,
more resonate than any trunk,
metallic and throaty,
its tone carrying out through
the Madrona trees and the blooming Rhodies.

Gleefully, he bends to his task,
finally loud and bold and sexy,
playing an instrument God had never designed
for his ancestors' quieter forest.

KBN

Dying without Imagination

Mentor, Mystic, Saint, Teresa of Avila, Sophia's voice,
I hear your wisdom. It arises in timely ways as the very
voice of God.

And yet lately…I turn your pages estranged. Who are you
when, "watch out" you say, "What you hear might be your
ego, the devil's voice, or *imagination.*" *Wait Teresa, I offer my
ego and weeds of devilish voices, but imagination? It must stay.*

I try to excuse and rationalize for you - semantics, culture,
the age, but I leave your *Interior Castle* closed, disappointed
that you betray Imagination, source of play, song, story,
wisdom- dark and light in well-placed silence and in poems.

A deep and quiet suggestion has me turn to your poetry and
there! You greet in a language I feel. You write, "the ego
takes sides, but the heart embraces all." Teresa, let me
embrace all of you.

How hard it must have been to write of spiritual things for
intellect, riven with ego. Your poetry speaks to the heart
while your prose sweat and threaten. I bow to your wily
survival for you wrote for men of power, friends of the
Inquisition. Their grandfathers paraded your father's father,
for being a Jew, naked through the streets, whose cobbled
stones wept for the shame of it all.

I imagine us reading poetry together in a secret place. Like you, I want to say, *I'm here!* when I hear spirit calling clear as my husband in the kitchen. I often say, *Speak Lord*, when imagination calls a poem to me. Teach me,
Saint Teresa, your skillful means. You learned sky, water and earth despite the confines of rules and rationality. You knew the poetic and faith-filled reality: we must head towards cliffs or sink into fathoms of despair. Our bones break and we suffocate if we forget to live in the truth of our imagination
...*we are the ocean, earth, and sky.*

SSH

Writing Life

My books climb up the wall,
over seven feet above my head,
(ground zero in an earthquake I'm thinking —
death by falling books fits me perfectly).
My office is so small that two butts wouldn't fit side by side.
But when I write, I turn my head to the thin window,
and gaze out on a fiberglass St. Francis
and a vast, old cedar tree.

That's enough of a view, really.

And music? Conan, Battlestar Galactica, the Eagle,
rousing soundtracks because
I don't do caffeine that much, just mainline the audio
like a kind of shaman drum high.

I like this little womb-room, though.
I am the anchoress of our house,
hearing Ian skyping with someone in Japan,
listening to Steve describe database design
to an *actual* rocket scientist
while I swim with a favorite character of mine
in an underground plant sanctuary
on a planet grown
gray and dead.

It's all just words, ephemeral, but
always, I am a kind of nun,

devoted to such mysteries,
raising my eyes to all those impossible books
and choosing to
write
life.

KBN

The Daffodil's Question
Creativity is the Holy Ghost. Brenda Ueland

Creativity - dominate trait of the Divine, calls me to till my
life of color. Trapped behind grey eyes, trudging up a hill,
I noticed a daffodil staring into my face with its fluted sun
and it seemed a question.

The generosity in its short extravagant life made me tender.
Stunned, I stopped. Its existence and implication, and oh –
the desire it raised. Mysterious teacher, it asked, *what
are you doing with beauty?*

Confused as Paul, knocked off his horse, I couldn't answer
why I let lie dormant creativity. A violence, a persecution ,
eeking an anemic life through arteries shriveled by lack of art.

I made an appointment with my Self to move creativity back
into my life. I would feel my way to friends of this Truth and
absorb healing until I could see the color of the Holy Ghost,
probably yellow.

SSH

Symphonic

So many words float,
symphonic —
I see the world through them,
all the different ways I can say "green".

A new Buddhist once said,
"Oh, a writer of fiction, you're *really* lost."

Maybe.

But then,
she's never held a novel character's hand,
cold-fingered after falling in a mountain creek,
ran her thumb over his broken nails,
and looked into eyes the same gray as ice,
depthless.

When such a one as this speaks,
I listen,
because he will have words
that are beyond this little conception
of
me.

KBN

Coloring

What happens when the words finally
stop,
and coloring to music seems enough--
oh, adult coloring for sure,
rich Arabic motifs or Celtic knots,
blues and greens and lightest yellows.
I dream of papering an entire wall,
living inside a mosque like
the Dome of the Rock in Jerusalem.

But coloring isn't inlaid tile after all,
just swipes from a plastic marker,
so I grin at such grandiose plans
for my kindergarten exercise.

The words? Well, they always seem to
come back,
if only to make meaning
colorful.

KBN

Fishers

More often than not I follow a gull with its irresistible arch
soaring across my mind. Then I miss the subtle tug from the
depths. It gets away. Sometimes I snag a dog fish, its back
cracked by the last fishermen who caught it, or a ball of
tangled kelp essentially becoming the day's slippery catch.

Fishermen and poets will tell you that what we do is about
being present to possibilities and surprises. I pull reel line,
yarding more and more until a long line of words bend
with the currents as it becomes a plumb line stretching
straight to the dark below. I stare into water with layers
of translucence melting into black, inviting me to imagine
what swims below. I feel the cutting skin of the shark,
tumble in displaced water swirling after a whale's fluke,
marvel at the grace of the jelly fish and the wisdom of octopi.

After a while poetry feels like breathing under water,
a life-line holding me to the air of my mystery.

SSH

Writing with Light

All the time
I want to write with light,
the way a winter sun can send tendrils
along the fern-spine and drip,
luminous
onto moss-hair and stone.
But the truth is, I also like the shadows,
the dark lines of the bark,
the crack in the shell,
the point in the water where
everything fades into mystery.
This is the season of the womb,
where words are known more by touch
and the candle-light
makes me sigh in wonder
as it glows in velvet darkness.

KBN

Strength of Pilgrims

As a writer, I rather enjoy the pilgrimage, the journey of putting words on the page and allowing rather than demanding the story of the passage to emerge. The plot grows out of the movement, out of the dance of the characters, and I am often simply a mute and wondering hiker among them. I suppose I trust the path the same way I know that when I step into a classical labyrinth, I can only go to the center of it all, despite the switchbacks of the internal critic, the edits, the feedback that stings. And that eventually, my characters and I will make our way back out toward the world, and standing at the entry and exit point of the ancient symbol, I will let them go. Let them go, yes, and know the next group of souls from within will beckon me back onto the path once more.

KBN

Dweller in the Heart

I got rejected today;
A baby of mine,
78,000 words or so,
turned away for not being quite
sexy enough.

But the character,
he laughed inside me,
peeking around the shadows of my heart,
shaking his head.
He will always be a warrior first,
lover second;
Would I change that for money?

Would I change anyone else in my life
for coin?

And if he,
of all shadowy men,
can find the humor in such things,
well,
who am I to brood?

KBN

Adolescent Art

Middle-school teens of every nationality bring their art
to this show, life-sized tape sculptures, rolling panels
laden with water colors, acrylic, charcoal, pencil, chalk,
tables covered with ceramic piggy banks of such expressions,
cockeyed-comical, teapots with jungle leafs and starfish.

All this here, in spite of the crime and poverty; seven police
park at the adjoining high school.

All this here, where parents, friends, teachers gaze at the art,
study the name, then look for their friend, their child, their
student with new admiration. Shy artists smile in response.

So many ways for children to be destroyed, but not here,
not today. They are strong with their art.

Karim from the Eastern bloc may one day be an illustrator
or a car mechanic - here he begins to learn access to his depth-
brilliant in any job.

Joshapreet from India will feel the heat of American and
Indian eyes; her art will water her confidence to grow
in both worlds.

Neusha, an Iranian girl of superior intellect, one day
an astrophysicist , perhaps…but her art connects her
to her true genius.

Addictions will chain the lives of some, but if they drink
freedom, it will come from the same well they drew this art,
from the divine in their depth.

SSH

Cycles and Paradox

*How wonderful that we have met with a paradox.
Now we have some hope of making progress.*

Niels Bohr

Core of Community

Rock becomes separated,
thrown out of the depths
by fire or
pried away from the mountain
by fingers of wind and rain.

Rock stands alone, one.

Then rock softens,
breaks down, dances
with the short-lived things
and leavings of creatures mobile
and ephemeral.

Rock is manyness.

Then a single seed drops,
nurtured in dark soil,
loose enough that rain can whisper
"grow up, grow down"
to its hardened shell.

Seed stands alone, one.

Some warmth reaching it,
beckoning,
finally touches something lonely within
and then, the seed cracks,
roots and stem unwind

from the singularity.

Seed is manyness.

Roots probe the spaces between
heaviness and lightness,
Each fingerling fiber alone,
each fingerling fiber manyness.

The stem reaches up
swiftly moving from standing alone
to wreathing itself with leaves,
a dancing, bobbing manyness.

And for each singular leaf,
the pattern fractures into veins,
the one and the many whirling
with life.

Until
finally,
a single flower bursts forth,
black center wreathed with golden petals.
Ripens in the one sun,
feeds from the many drops of rain.
Roots cracking rocks,
nesting,
dropping a single seed
into the arms of community.

KBN

The Maple

There by Kyoto's gold temple, we pick up a seed
of a maple tree, and place it in the center of a tissue,
my husband folds and places in his pocket. The temple
gleams on mounds of moss, reflected clear on a blue lake.
On its shore, gardeners bend under bamboo hats, floating
celestial and pointed mountains. Fine fingers pick needles
and leaves one by one, spent but burning yellow and red.

We place that idea of a tree in home soil where it grows
from sprout to whip to elegant heights lighting the world
with its green glow or torching skies of Northwest grey
with Kyoto's radiant gold. In spring, I revel in its lacey green,

but autumn finds me meager in felt praise as I resist winter,
resenting the way it bleeds the tree, leaving only black veins.
Wanting to love it all, I argue with my heart – *fall leaves deserve
the same adoration as their youth.* I lean over my laptop to view
this long member of the yard, see it brighten dark forest edge,
feel a suggested compromise of praise. Sadness can love
autumn as joy holds the spring. I bow to its before-life
and after death-resurrection.

SSH

One-to-Two-to-One

Along the single stem of the fern,
the flat, elongated leaves pair up,
marching down the spine to the tiniest
singular tip,
a triangular tongue sipping the breeze.
Out of the riled waves,
a rare gray whale breaches
and falls into mystery again.
The dead mouse is eaten by the chicken,
who in turn,
lays my breakfast — see it now
two-one-two-one
like breathing,
like fire.

KBN

Imagine

never seeing an image of yourself
(and already you can catch the pun)
just the
occasional laugh,
the feathered kiss,
or the rib-breaking hug,
the spoon touching your lips,
the water, cool, swallowed on a hot day,
the earth damp and black under your nails,
the drum-beat in your breast bone,
the smell of the young lily of the valley,
the stars overhead when
the world presses too tightly.

Where is the "you" in all of this?
Simply everywhere, my friend.

KBN

Beach Powers

Rising over the last dune, "Ah" rumbles up her throat as
tumblers foam at the earth's edge; immensity opens her.

She turns away from dark and distant silhouettes of people,
breathes through her mouth near the dead whale, melted by
time into mounds of formless fat, ripe under the webbed feet
of gulls humped in a shrug. She is one more in the summer's
train of people, constant and curious about death and size
while the harbor seal curious but shy, dives seeing
she returns its gaze.

She imagines Jino, a local poet and fisherman with rock-star
appeal, to be the one-man crew of the boat trawling off shore.
His rhymes make her love ordinary things like tea-cups of
bone china on diesel boats, make her forget the labor of her
exercise, invite her to play with an image of her holding one
end of a great net while the fisher poet holds the other. They
drag it netting silvery and willing catch.

Turning round, she sees on closer view the dark, small people
are in fact, great white pelicans which lift in elegant formation
as she nears. The empty air beneath such size amazes her,
raises her eyes like morning clouds that scud heavy with
longing and brilliant with hope.

She turns towards the dunes, steps over logs that shore up
sand, patterned with daisy tracks of some small scurrying.
Seeing this testament of a small belonging grows her
in this home of giants.   SSH

Stealer of Hearts

The door was cracked, just a bit,
so she could hear the falling rain
and the smell of lilacs —
or maybe the goat and sheep pens
were even more enticing.
I imagine she shoved the door wide,
lingered, sniffing a thousand things
humans never notice.
Her arthritic legs stiff,
she strolled out to
roll in the little nodules of vegetarian poo,
covering her own scent,
an intuition from the times of need,
when the blood ran hotter
and knew how to give chase.
Once cloaked in such anonymity,
one new scent led to another
(it was nothing personal)
until she could no longer hear
the sharp whistle and clap
of her special strange two-legged pack members —

how the game trails still call,
wet, lush and young with spring,
unaware that they are the stealer of hearts.

KBN

Rain Dancing

Picked ripe plums yesterday
and the last of the blueberries,
wove the final passes of a prayer shawl,
said goodbye to a friend for six weeks—
she is chasing the sun,
while I wait for the clouds and rain.
Ninety degrees today,
but the light slants golden
right after dinner now,
and the calls of the birds grow hoarse.
The foghorns, too, cry out over the water,
giving voice to that itchy place where
warm dampness and cold collide,
twisting up summer wraiths,
on their way to becoming something else,
rain-dancing
among the tree-tops.

KBN

Light and Darkness

A shaft of light cuts
through dark forest
beaming the fir trunk
and low salal in light
as at center stage.

July's afternoon glows
through lace curtain
that blocks it just so,
knitting a rose shadow
on the wall by my bath,
cheered by this tapestry
dancing shadow lines.

The light scatters too.
Ten thousand gems
ride the ridges of the bay
blown into sparkling chaos.

A convicted teenager,
tells how he murdered
a transient under the bridge.
Then he confesses his dream,
to be a doctor, smart and able
to help poor people. I cry
for the boy's innocent little
light on the blue screen.

The moon, a round pearl
shines white
in the great darkness
that holds this orb
tender, so as not
to overcome her–
so in need
of the other
are they, this
darkness and light.

SSH

Spun but not Dried

Spin these cycles round again,
the seed to plant to seed,
the egg to hen to egg,
the nut to tree to nut,
and when your mind reaches out
to stop that glorious
spiraling
creative
breathing of the universe,
remember
fence lines and
walls
lines of words
and moats of thought,
all must one day swirl away
in stardust.
Endings are for those
who are a little afraid
of
their
beginnings...
so
spin these cycles round again
and this time
laugh
out-loud.

KBN

Source of Amazement

Sound-side,
I like snuggling down into
rocks and broken shells,
the sun baking the seaweed into
Nori-smells.
Rooted, I can take the smallest grain
of a volcano in my hand,
see all its facets and sheen,
then blow it, lyrical,
into the curl of a wave.
Amazement:
small and intimate.

KBN

Of Other Worlds

She travels in the dark
to the wilderness of her dreams
behind eyelids fluttering faster
than both the rhythm of her heart
beating an easy pace going where she will
or racing -going where she wouldn't.
The bear, caged by day, roams roaring
and rooting his nose in the dirt of night
disturbing a truth that has softened
with memory and wonder which makes
it ripe and ready in this world to pick.
This is the way to tend darkness and
waken the mother of the soil world,
who quietly nurses white roots that reach,
blind and trusting, downward in warmed soil.
In time, she will release the green shoot
as she trusts her offspring to the unknown
above, where they sprout awake into the light.

SSH

Fluidity

Cooler morning,
fog-drenched ribbons of green
twist silver droplets
into finery
for no particular reason.

I like it when my eyes are windows
instead of walls,
when I can hear God in the garden,
walking,
and that's all that matters,
not making sense of it,
just being
the granola
the almond milk
the steam of the coffee.
Allaha means both yes and no,
light and dark,
full and empty.
Hard to take any stand
on such paradox,
better to just move as it does,
fluid,
bird-wings and water washing
empty shells.

KBN

Drifting Mist

Saturate us today,
moisturize our woodeness,
oil our stiff places,
link us drop by drop, woven
in a veil that shimmers
between the stone and tree,
the candle and the wave,
sunshine and clay.
And let us become pliable,
but not naïve,
snakes and doves
intertwined,
droplets glimmering
on feather and scale
gemlike
but ephemeral —
until we understand the
dampness in our own eyes--
eternal.

KBN

The Restorer

The sun bleached shelves
held ceramic cats waving
their glazed paws through dust,
candles circled with wreathes
of plastic leaves lost their glitter,
a cloud of orange- specks of light,
everywhere magazines strewn
with faded pictures, some of boys
 in striped t-shirts pulling red-flyers.

The force of the wind surprised
the shopkeeper–stymied meteorologists.
How could a wind blow so localized
to slam through one store's window,
scattering its inventory into one pile?

For the shop keeper's part, at first dazed,
she stood by the debris with a strange lightness,
found herself liking the light, the dark film
of greased panes gone and the living air
of the fresh world outside now in.

SSH

Holy Trinity!

I fought it a long time;
I cut my theological teeth
on Jesus Christ Superstar,
and was in love with Spock —
how could I *not* argue,
logically speaking?

Not a bad place to start —
holy sex appeal and pure rational thought
mixed creatively in the bowl of a teenage girl,
its own potent trinity I suppose,
and better because
I couldn't see it then.

Satchitanada--
It's the way I know it now,
being, consciousness and bliss
or
Father as ground of being,
Son as our experienced world
Holy spirit as that sense
of flowing movement, and
that all shall indeed be well.

Logically intuitive, in the end.
And no less sexy.

KBN

Labyrinth of Mercy

I didn't step into a tidy circle
at journey's start, rather I slipped
squalling into hands I made bloody.

And I still cry out wandering
circuits of every direction,
out and in, smug in seasons
where I can almost touch center,
terrified when centrifugal force
flings me out to what feels lost.
But you, Merciful One, and I

are like grandpa and the tabby.
He rubbed her orange back
with his arthritic hands, laughed
low and tender as his visitor pranced
her paws slow, arched her back
in the pleasure of connection.
She followed him out and down
the trailer steps and went on living
her cat life without looking back.

SSH

Mystery

The world is more mysterious than we believe.

Huston Smith

Christ

Sometimes, this word still stops me in my tracks. Jesus, Yeshua, these are names I understand, human and imperfect, companionable, ever ripening. But *Christ*, that is a symbol, an abstract, a title that stands as a mask before the man who was close enough to God to call him Abba. It is not until I experience that I *share* in that consciousness, that state of being, that I move closer to understanding the relationship Yeshua had with God. For Christ is the transpersonal term, the Name that calls us all into involution, process and paradox.

KBN

Illumined One

Why this rock?
I knelt and picked it up from the shoreline,
its face barnacled in miniature,
its black body shot through with lines of white.
One among so very many,
yet it alone spoke to me.
Illuminated world!
Each step we take is really
full of light and shouts and flags waving
but what mystery makes us blobby, fleshy humans
zero in, slow our minds enough
to allow ourselves to be bent and lengthened
and thinned like rays of light?
The only answer today:
black stone, white inclusions, barnacles.

Or maybe, just another question--
where is your rock?

KBN

Physician

God save me
from every person who knows
this naturopath,
that miracle herb,
this surgeon,
that new test.

No, I don't mean
such folks are somehow
separate from You,
and I am sure
each, in their appointed time,
felt Your breath inside of them
and met another
right at the moment they should
and were healed.

Miracles happen in such loose ways.

But what I need today
is simply
Thy will be done —
a careful ear tending the everyday
a not-knowing smile and shrug
that says
come out and see!
A new cherry tomato has ripened
in a land of cloud and cool rain.
Let us take and taste
sunshine and tart splashes
of life.

Physicians,
like miracles,
show up in
such
loose
ways.

KBN

Kingdom Come

How can I prepare the ground?
Haunting, is it not,
to rip away the tattered leaves and
dead, twinning roots,
brush aside the ant and slug,
and run fingers into mystery
until fingernails are caked and broken.
But then, after all this effort,
this me-energy expended ,
the bird drops a single seed in a
careless
intuitive
random gesture-
the tiny hint of a tree
that will, in its perfectly
careless
intuitive
random way
open its arms for the same bird's weary body.
Is this not the Kingdom come
at last?

KBN

The Small, Single Flame

Let the out-breath go,
pushing your skin large,
breaking the connection between
brain and
eye
and
ear
where the tangle of the blackberry bush
finally loses its thorns
where the water warms then dissipates at your touch
where even the swirl of galaxies cannot hold you
and yet, you can still dwell
as a small, single flame
in a human's beating heart.

KBN

A Good Losing

There is a good losing
when you are the one lost,
absorbed in the present,
blessed state of wonder
hidden from *self*-consciousness.

Once I forgot myself
in the most unlikely of places:
singing alone at the center
of a circle of people.

Who doesn't fantasize
about performing
with abandon?

I did this singing…
experimental,
improvisational,
goofy,
wildly creative,
and connecting.

Hours flew like minutes
as I floated words and notes
coming from I-don't-know-where.

Lost in love with music,
with the other singers,
with the musician within me,
 I met the joy and mystery
of losing myself.
Now I seek this losing,
knowing
it is the pearl
in the night.

SSH

Breath of Life

It is pretty ephemeral you know,
the stories I write,
the poetry
the words, even the gestures,
lost in a moment,
data-streams like photons,
racing away from me,
particle, wave, bye-bye.
And yeah, sometimes
they collide with someone
swirl around and dance a bit,
then shoot off in another direction.

Ever tried to hold the light?
It's like breathing in, breathing out.

KBN

Moving Mists

roll across a flat bay
the bow of a fishing boat
chugs through their fog,
which softens the sight
of its hull, muted
like a water color.

On land this cloud
waters the poppy
on the cliff's edge,
where beads of water
magnify its crepe curve
of textured red petals.

This mist shrouds
and reveals
the mystery
of the land
we think we know
on a clear day.

SSH

Source

I played chicken and egg a lot as a child,
particularly those sticky summer days
when I lay wheezing in my bed,
staring at a long poster of the rise
of dinosaurs.
In a glance, I could see their progression —
trilobite to T-Rex
and then
it happened--
a small, fuzzy rat thing
peeking out beneath the ferns.
What a surprise she must have been
to her smooth-skinned mama:

She *ate* eggs, after all.

KBN

Gracious Creator

Soft falls the morning sunshine,
sunshine-sparked dust-motes hang unapologetic.
Unapologetic, I run my finger through it all
all of It, the very breath of life,
life upheld on particle and wave
waves, drifting round me,
me, blazing like the sun.

KBN

Pardon Me

Really, it's quite selfish.
Just open your heart enough
so that the river of life can flood through,
carrying away the gnarled root
and black tar of your stuck places
until
that compost left behind,
rich and wriggling and alive,
will make you gasp,
tickling up between your spread toes.

The anonymous World War One poet
knew that lively rush:
it is in pardoning that
we
are
pardoned.

KBN

Abba!

Abba I have cried you--
those times when I needed a compass
a listening ear.
It wasn't wrong, to name you thus,
to fling "daddy" to the universe
and feel the sense of being
carried, held, and heard.
But sometimes
Abba teases apart in the wild wind
dancing the fir trees,
or
gets lost in the script
of the stars,
stretched out thin and broad.
The secret beyond the name?
This silent lump in my heart and throat
is
still
holy.

KBN

Bible Train

To leave slavery, you ask us
to clutch our chains like Samson,
blind, but strong enough to pull
down pillars bracing prison walls.

You ask us to sit before Deborah,
take her hard council to face power
with trust in our being enough.
Your angel of destruction takes care
of the rest in Jael, who lures oppressors
with warm milk, invites them in her tent,
then steps out holding a bloody head.

Dazed by death that stuns our life,
your hands rest upon our shoulders,
turn us towards our work of building

each our own holy temple with Solomon's zeal,
to sneak into Boaz's bed with Ruth's creativity,
to birth Christ with Mary as midwife,

the Angels, for their part, sing their cheers of *Yes*.

SSH

Dark Night

The dark will be your womb tonight.

David Whyte

Scratching

The lab is wearing the cone of shame today;
it's allergy season and she thinks
if she can skin herself with her teeth,
get through the hair and skin to the blood
and dig it all out,
all will be well.

I know how she feels;
I rub at my own skin-deep hot patches.

Peace walkers trudge by on the highway,
drumbeats and flags.
They are itchy, too, I think,
and scratching in their own way.

I can move nature around in my garden
the big visible bits, anyway
dig out the weeds
(some that I would raise as houseplants in Michigan),
water here,
fertilize there,
lay in a spiral of stone.

But still,
the maples are turning now,
spiders moving indoors,
and tomorrow and then the next day,
the clouds will mute all this riotous green.

We scratch in dust,
all of us.

KBN

Come Here

Throw out the image of flags
and pep rallies and
weapons hoisted overhead
in strong fists.
Come into this little sun-drenched room
and watch the finches at the feeder,
bright yellow with spring finery,
so busy with their bits of millet.
Suddenly they flee as one,
blurred golden photons to the budding oaks,
as the shadow passes
silent,
predatory wings etched on the green grass
like a shudder.
Breathless, the wait, the stillness.
And then, one by one,
in flashes of mating splendor they gather,
swoop down on their feast
millet tossed in praise,
visiting beak to beak about how death
scooped so close,
When? Where?

How quickly they go back to the basics:
this good food,
this fine water,
that lovely female, waiting,
her eyes bright with shy wonder.
Listen when the birds sing of real freedom.

KBN

Between Storms

The rain flung with a raging wind
beats against the pane and matches
my pain; for balance I breathe
from toe to head with the furnace
blowing steady. I feel its chant.
The storm wraps my sadness, gives
relief. Likewise, when the wind
drops, I feel what I do not want.
The radio alarm clicks and faint
strings play, bright and startling
in their thinness. The air in my lungs
arriving, leaving soothes the gut
like a painter stroking comfort
in slow swaths of blue – a moment
and eternity between winter storms.

SSH

Angels of the Shadows

Notice the angels of the shadows,
those frozen snapshots of
human-shaped marble lintels,
of doorways,
of thin places,
their wings half-spread, their gaze,
always down-ward toward the earth.

I pull up, and pull in,
and wonder
at the itch between
my own shoulder-blades.

Their eyes are cold up-close,
sometimes without a carved pupil
to create near and far,
dark and light for them.
Maybe that's how they walk *between*,
their stillness asking us
to shatter stone
with our imaginations
and
see the light in the darkness.

KBN

A Neuron's Mirror

Most days,
I can feel life all around me,
from the stone's nest to the breeze-blush,
from leaf to damp green slug,
vibrations from the lyre,
my son's deepening laughter.

But then there are days
when I want a name
to whisper
a presence to walk along with,
concrete, brand-named, crowd-approved
you know all the possible personalities,
all those consensual constructs —
see, I can't quite bring myself
to believe such things.
This wanting, though,
it's not born of wakefulness, not really,
more like catching a scent of something from childhood
and having only impressions of arms and safety.
Or finding a card from 1897, words of love
scratched in ink, but that is all.
More like an itch,
and all the yoga postures in the world
won't make me flexible enough
to give it a good scratch.
And there is nothing of cowardice here,
buried in this longing,
to breathe with the divine in a human form--

maybe only a lonely brain cell,
short dendrites reaching
for some kind of a mirror.

KBN

Visiting with Tears

My sister told me she felt the presence
of Grandmother Winifred, grieved by her
short life dying at age thirty-six unable

to deliver her eighth child alive, grieved
that her children grew motherless.
I shivered at the story of this apparition.

Why, I wondered, *wasn't grandma in
a cloud of witnesses seeing the rightness
of life beyond the living?*   I summoned

the crying ghost by whispering,
"Grandma, I expected you to see beyond
the living. How sad you grieve your fate.

Wouldn't it be better to send us means
to break the hardpan-lie that we live
insignificant lives? Grandma, you know

I suffer seasons when I hate my finiteness,
mediocrity, inability to unlink the chains
of wounding I cause and receive. You know

how I plug my ears against that ticking,
announcing as I imagine a shrill bell ringing:
times up, life over! Today I cried my prayers

because of you. I need you, sad ghost, to stop

your head-hanging, your moaning that life
was not enough. How hard to believe we matter.

Grandma, a silence full of prayer and tears
rested my fears that you might be right. Instead,
I was invited to enter the sky through holes

of passing clouds to stand with you. I watched
our patch of blue grow vast and calm in a blue reality,
dissolving the mirage of insufficiencies, unlocking

prisons of how we think life should go. We traveled
then to a cliff, banked on the Straights of Juan de Fuca,
where winds pushed and blazed us forward.

You stood next to me with your children, theirs,
and mine breathing dignity, chins up, knowing
life is enough. We watched you see that cloud

of witnesses celebrating above - celebrating
your short life, lived well enough. You left, and
we knew you would stop visiting with tears.

SSH

Al-Ghanni

I hold my hand against my chest.
It hurts today, that place
where half of my stomach pushed beyond
its natural limits through a small hole.
I wonder what it is trying to say,
one organ to another —
no food gets up above the diaphragm
but oh,
acid and carbonation always rise.

There is a poem in that, too, I am sure.

What is it whispering about there,
this separate chunk of my stomach,
framed by ribs, tapped at by my heart
massaged by my lungs?
Can't it feel where its tissue is being rubbed raw
with each movement of breath?

Perhaps it does not quite understand,
boundaries are not to cage out or cage in,
but to cook us, contain us, focus us —
ecstasy erupts from the very pressure of the veil,
the open garden will be eaten by deer,
except for the parts made of stone.

KBN

I Fight with You Sometimes—

digging in my feet hard,
until I can just about ridge up the carpet,
leaning back to hold the door shut and
keep
You
out.
Yeah, as if You aren't already "in" —
it's just...
it's just..
well, it's dusty in here,
the dog threw up on the carpet again,
the dishes have piled up
and all the flowers in the windowsill are dead.
Yeah, they're bulbs, so I can put them in the earth
and they'll pop back up next year.

But still...

Navaho women say you can't leave a loom empty
for more than three days, or
the spirit will leave it,
like a corpse.
You watched as I gave away all my weaving stuff—
looms, carders, wheel and shuttles
all waiting on the front porch today
to come to life in someone else's hands.
Rebirth for that which has given me joy —
and good news for some homeless spider-spirits, I suppose.

I put my sheep on Craig's List.
Goats, too.
I'm eyeing the pond, thinking the goldfish
might enjoy taking their chances
with the heron and raccoon.
The dogs? No chance—my son would track them down
and bring them home again.
They know how to say "I love you" day after day,
with just their eyes.

At least I haven't sheared my hair short,
penance for something I can't even name.
Maybe because there's all the other cutting coming--
pull the stomach down from my chest,
tighten the lower sphincters up,
and just how much more money can
I throw at the big, gray hospital anyway?

At least the surgeon can go to Ireland this year, right?
Well, hell.

You see, sometimes I get tired of my own company,
of trying to be
just so
just so I can eat, sleep and be enough,
and wish karma away
for another day,
even though it's riding my shoulders like
a prayer shawl.
OK, the door's unlocked,
might as well come in--

fresh towels in the bathroom anyway,
and maybe you can recline and sing to me for a while
about blue skies
and delicate meadow daisies,
and laugh about how ducks love to eat slugs
until their little bills get glued shut.

I'll try my best to take the hint.

KBN

The Living Word for One

I wonder if the mind of Jesus wandered,
as even the evolved would in human pain;
Jesus was hanging, after all, nailed to a cross.

As a word-person, might he not have listed words
of alliteration as a way to take his mind from pain?
Words like crux, crash, crunch, creep, crap, or crass,

which would lead him back through the fog
to recall how this cramping world hangs Christs
on crosses. Maybe in the midst of his despair,

thinking God wasn't sobbing and had abandoned
him to unbearable pain of body and good-bys,
he couldn't see that his vertical heart touched

heaven already and his outstretched arms
embraced all creation. Now in pain-less paradise,
Jesus, still a word person, ponders which new words

the world needs like one for death and life,
lose and find, now and later, within and without
intimate and infinite, loved, loving, and beloved,

in other words, a new word for one.

SSH

Forgiver

Gift, it is, this rare word,
wordlessly given, like tea in a cup
cupping warmth and liquid mystery
mysteries, birthing from dry leaf and water
watering what should have been death,
deathly stillness, when eye lifts
uplifting a heart too long guarded,
oh Guardian, ever renew and forgive
the forgiver.

KBN

Blushing Words

They stacked the journals by the fire,
years of words,
galaxies of confusion and anger and depression
scalding
and also the little joys of birds at the feeder,
delicate figurines in a glass case,
rows of preserves, neatly labeled, all that
tucked in around the edges.

She had died,
and her oldest child, reading
found a mother he did not know.
What we cannot bury,
we burn.

KBN

Gracious Gardener

I'm not setting out today
to make neat rows,
or ease the tender plant
into a bed of soft, black earth.
Today, I want to come with a sharp hoe,
rip out weeds
toss the head-sized rocks in a pile
the sound of their clashing
carried out over the broad field.
I want it all in piles,
where I can see it,
mingled with my sweat,
the bones of the past,
and what I am making of them.

KBN

The First Sun

It's worth the wait;
the forest green like a simple 2-D movie
flares into rounder form with the sun,
shadow and light,
the firs tipped with their new growth,
as if a wild manicurist had visited
in the night.

I have lived in lands of sun-
Texas, Australia, Nebraska.
But it never struck me so lovely
as the spears of light stabbing
into the gloom,
flaring along moss
leaping
on the curving waves of the Sound
like a child at play.

People say the clouds here are depressing,
the long dark of winter, confining.
But oh, are we not taught the wonder
of patience by our still and expectant land?

KBN

Shekinah

You showed yourself
in the lumbering bear
that kept crossing
my path as I was running,
driving, or looking
out my kitchen window.
I knew you, ferocious
mother, guarded my heart
that hard, good year.

SSH

Of Horses and Hospitals

Mechanical bed,
pastel blanket,
five tubes,
FIVE, I counted several times,
falling asleep sometimes between
three and four,
and a clock that didn't seem to understand
how time works--
it rhythmically destroyed one-thousand-one
to skip or
slide to a sticky halt.
I expected, prayer beads sliding between my
weak fingertips,
a sense of angels,
a rescue by a mystical blue glow or maybe
at least
powerful, thrilling insight...
but no...
only the feel of a muzzle against my hand,
long whiskers tipped with ice,
the nicker of recognition,
fuzzy-coated, mud spattered,
and the smell!
Hay and earthy warmth.

Perhaps at thin places,
all our intellectual practices must bow
before the real heaven
our animal bodies once found,
and carry stubbornly in our bones.

KBN

Razor Edge

The razor edge defines
the path between
surrender and
depression.

I mean,
surrender is useful, clean;
it scrapes away old paint,
peeling the dry chips from
solid wood in little curls of color,
while depression gets the stuff
under your fingernails,
little gouging runnels
aimless and random.

Surrender can cut out the finest line drawing,
following curve and angle
and mistakes, well, they become part of the pattern,
do-overs, giggles and "lets begin again"
just steps on the journey.
Depression knows only the straight line,
forced up into a corner into something solid,
where not yielding feels noble somehow.

OK, you get the point--
and the edge as well.

KBN

Pool of Mercy

Like water,
meditation seeps into the cracks,
drawn to the low places,
the sticky dark spots.
Breath by breath,
the shadowy bits rise;
they cannot abide the silence,
the stillness,
the drip-drip-drip of lungs,
filling and emptying.

But lifting them into the air
throwing them into the light?

Tears, my friends!
Some of it will ride on tears,
from the pool of mercy.

KBN

The Source of All

At church today I see my friend wobble in weakness
in her hard walk of dying. I hate this turn. A chaplain
tells during coffee hour of a boy, nineteen, bright and
trapped, born to a gang, forced to torture or die himself,
imprisoned, solitary confinement. I think of Lily, fourteen,
coming to school unbathed. Classmates deride this child
of a homeless addict. She stops attending and now as they
say, walks the Ave. Source of All, this pain presses my lungs.
I cannot breathe.

I wonder how You, Source of Compassion, hold us, each
and every child, human and beautiful, old and young. How
do you look and not implode from the blackness, even you
sucked inside? Since I trust your love more than my breath,
something tenuous guesses, imagines, clings to a truth,
my root of life confident that you must see differently.

Perhaps you see now and later when our suffering turns
to beauty. Do you consort with the broken hearted in a way
that allows them to see what is more real than pain? I need
this way of seeing. If we are to care and survive, we need
to see as you see, to love as you love.

SSH

The Consoler

He will not let me
hold him when he is ill;
he shuts the door between us,
firmly
I hear him
drawing covers over his slim shoulders.

I can only whisper two words through
variegated wood and metal locks:
"I'm here."

KBN

Moon's Grace

Lord, I am weary today,
the light on snow hurting my eyes,
the dim roar of the traffic
invading the taste of my eggs.
Halloween cobwebs cease to charm
where they float near the ceiling.
As the first green shoots vie with cold white,
I want to huddle,
I want to curve one bear-paw over my snout,
live off the fat of berries and salmon a while longer.
Yes, I am vast and heavy,
dense and bitter as darkest chocolate,
and even the robin flicking bits of leaf to the wind,
barely tickles a smile from me.
But enough of such things,
dip the teabag, breathe steam.
Healer, help me understand,
I am tidal, and today
though sunk back into a place
of empty shells
I will be lifted again
as the moon's grace calls me forth.

KBN

The Subduer

The mare stood calm to my touch,
but her foal, shy, slipped under her.
When he grew too big for that route,
I spread my arms corralling him
against her flank. I cupped hands
round his shoulder and butt, scratched
his chest, rubbed his hips
till one day, he stayed near.

Like that day, my bullied child,
white with rage, stormed inside;
I wrapped my arms around him
and held him in his frenzy 'til
he calmed. Our hearts beat
as one, our breath came and
went in unison. We sat close,
and I read aloud a good while.

This touch that subdues,
I need it today.
I want to lean calm,
pressing close to you,
hearing a good story.

SSH

Kenosis

*In my opinion, this practice costs per T.S. Elliot,
'no less than everything.'*

Cynthia Bourgeault

The Enricher

I sat a long time today,
staring out my widow,
overgrown black bamboo
catching and dribbling
light off the ends
of thin ribbons of green.

I struggled with this word "enrich"
my word to wrestle with before
yoga and pool and writing all began
and
images of white bread,
soy milk,
pastel colored cereals
kept popping up--
Plastic interruptions of my reverie.

And then I got it,
that one ah-ha for the day —
enrich is not something added,
but rather all the extraneous
taken away.

KBN

Sword and Lyre

Under the brilliant Washington sun-
yes, in July such things occur-
I watched my teenager lift his shield,
his sword angled just so,
facing off with another young man.

No matter that the helm was plywood,
the weapon merely rattan wrapped with-
get this-
a piece of a *yoga mat*-
I knew what they felt,
that warrior blood rising
without Halo or WOW,
twitching fingers curled
on reality and fantasy all at once.

I stopped strumming my Anglo-Saxon lyre,
seeing them both framed like that,
mountains rising behind,
lanky boys who needed to shave,
circling each other,
serious, cold,
before closing with a solid WHOP!
Laughing then, limbs thrown open,
miming death beneath the huge blue sky.

KBN

Broken

Two sides to this, as with all holy paradox
the empty teacup that makes room
for the new flavor;
the empty fireplace,
awaiting the spark;
the empty stall;
echoing with hoofed possibility;
the empty computer screen,
brilliant as full moon.

But also,
the halls of a house
after a death;
the egg shell crumbling
on the compost pile;
word of a text,
dated by culture and time;
the glass spice container,
forever scented with saffron.

Still,
the emptiness that eagerly accepts
and the emptiness that seems to hold ghosts,
are
the same thing, different mind.

KBN

Bending

I can remember the movie spin-off
of the *Thorn Birds*,
the young priest,
face down,
arms spread before the crucifix
the sleeves of his robe flared
like angel wings over the marble.

And for one breathless moment,
the rest of the plot simply did not matter.

I wanted to lie down beside him,
tip his head and try to feel
that sensual need to bare himself so,
the statue above,
staring down and through him,
something moving
in the stone.

Even as a child,
I could not bend like that.

KBN

Consolation

Don't grieve. Anything you lose
comes round in another form.

Rumi

The Consoler

When I cried over the loss of childish dreams,
where I rode the lead in my posse of admiring followers,
when I cried amazed that car wrecks break my bones too,
and when I, disappointed that my husband was neither prince
nor savior, my children not a supreme race, nor my art
brilliant, my ability to love, anemic and my claim to spiritual
eyes - only sometimes true, you soothed with the dove's coo,
heated the bath, rang the phone held in the hand of a friend,
wept from the heart's bleeding flower, wrapped me
in the embrace of a patient man. You asked me to love what
you loved, love it the best I could, love all and everything,
including me…the best I could.

SSH

The Patient One

Perhaps you have felt it:
that inkling that you could point
at Mount Rainier, riding red and huge
in the sunset
and tell it to attend you.
Heady thing, that,
a mountain at your beck and call.

But so much effort!
Seeing the tower of rock framed by sky,
imagining it drifting over the Sound
to crush the Wal-Mart parking lot.

Yes, it's OK to giggle at your creation.

Stand here with me for a moment,
watch the color drain away into blue shadows,
until mountain and cloud and ocean
sigh in your heart.

Did you not both come to heel?
Is this not the gift of patience?

KBN

The One Who Hears All

You hear the crumbs of soil give way
to the burrowing beetle,
the flick of a goat's ear in clear air
on a ridge, magnified green.
You hear droplets moving in a cloud,
the lids in ocean caves of blinking octopi,
the fetal thought, the wonder of the passing,
the dismay of the abused, the despairing crack
of the sentenced heart.

You hear our buried song, waiting for enough quiet
for us to hear it too and to ride the sound waving
in our watery and stony places of mystery,
first a rumble, then vibrations that shift the plates
of our foundation, quake in our chest, rattle our throat,
shake our mouths open with the continuation
of that first note, humming *ahhh*, singing awe,
kneading us soft into the breast

of the One who Hears All.

SSH

Castle of Resistance
—I am aware of what tempts me from the good.

Behind each swig of coke or each chunk of chocolate,
within each violent movie or book,
there is a rush, an energy,
a moment of I AM ALIVE
that often feels jittery, sad, alone
as chemistry becomes byproducts becomes
embarrassed awareness.

Yes, I know my warrior self very well,
understand how the yogi can also walk the way of the sword,
the qigong instructor write so easily of taking life
along the pulled bow of the sentence.

I resonate deeply with Arjuna's experience of the face of god,
teeth red with the bodies of fallen warriors,
all humanity streaming forth into the
end of flesh
and the beginning of waking.

For You are there,
ever present,
waiting to be noticed like the ground beneath my feet,
and when I fall,
moss-like, You enfold me again and again
and yet again
green, cool and brilliant.

KBN

Rest

...our heart is restless until it finds its rest in thee.

Augustine

After Honesty

Tenderness coos the soothe-song of the dove,
swaddles my flailing heart in furs, flings
petals floating above the flower-girl's wonder,
waves vines of honeysuckle in a warm breeze,
massages the knots in my shoulders with strong hands,
and smoothes the fret-lines burrowed in my forehead.

If only I could remember the nature of this rest next time
I freeze before choices that leave me clutching the rope-rails
of a thin bridge, swaying between high cliffs.

SSH

The Holy Trinity

Confused by the trinity, I asked the poor minister,
"Should I pray to Jesus, the Holy Ghost, or God?"
He had a quick answer before last seen on a stretcher
after collapsing at the pulpit looking angry to me,
a fourteen year old girl…mad, to the adults shaking
their heads. *To God through Jesus,* he answered though
even as a kid, I suspected neither one of us understood.
Wasn't I disloyal to pray to one and not the other?
And the alternative? I never liked four-way conversations.

Zen flower arrangement taught me the art of three,
where I reveled and rested in the aesthetics of space
between the branches showing
heaven,
sky,
and earth.

Let's relax if God be three, ten, or a thousand branches;
there is room to rest.

SSH

Beloved

Have you ever received
one of those
"pass this on to twelve other people"
emails?
I squirm when I get them.
Not because the intent isn't good.
Not because reaching out,
social cohesion
and
positive thinking
aren't all wonderful,
but
I'm working on something
small and sort of tight in my chest-
can I just sit with you, Beloved,
and notice the long grass in the lawn,
the cedar droppings on the porch,
the garden weeds and faded blooms
and be willing
to just be still with you?
I want that to be the greatest action
I take today
because that's something
I
can
pass
on.

KBN

Mystery

Omnipotent,
Reality
Sacred Truth...
these names for you
stretch me high and far
leaning way over the rail,
risking a fall. This I do
in respect and desire
to touch, see, taste,
a great Good,
much bigger
than me.
But I tire
of the strain
and curl up to rest
with you, Beloved
in that spoon shape,
holding, held, deep,
and near – embracing
not knowing which
is You or me
humming an Arabic song
of love, loving, and beloved.

SSH

Puttering

I've never learned the art of puttering,
that kind of doing that sputters and coughs
hesitates to awkward stops. I am like a toy,
with springs wound tight. Set me on a flat floor,
aim me at the task and let me focus and do,
always doing.

***

A friend at the close of her energetic life
called her slowing a reprieve, freedom
from the slave driver of constant going.
Her dying words follow me above my head
as I march through my day. I want her rest
before pronounced formally as "dying".

***

I had a vision of a toy car with a wind-up key,
jutting as a spear from its blue trunk. On its box
"directions to *dis*assemble: 'remove key, pry
open body, stretch coiled spring, leave toy
outside in rain.'" Now I visit toy stores resolved
to find such a car, totem of the unreasonable driver
who won't let up. I'll leave it to rust on a boulder,
solid, next to a pond still and rippling in season.

SSH

Guardian of my Deepest Self

I relieve you of command now;
go, where echoes and shadows play.
Don't worry! I'll be fine,
for the trees are in bloom
and the tide is in full and roaring
over the rocks.

There is nothing to guard here.
Contraction even to a self
is still a prison—
watch how the crow plays with the wind
his chest wide,
the ends of his wings conducting
an unseen music.

I'll play hide and seek with you later,
among the trees strung with moss
and where the trillium shade into dying pink.
But for now, I dare you
to clothe yourself in sky.

KBN

Encourager in the Night

Light gives way to dark,
embers' fade to gray,
dog's paws flutter dreaming
of coyotes; my husband warms
the bed waiting for me, but restless,
I scan the quiet for affirmation:
was the day used well? This day
of the ordinary? Of lighting the fire,
watching trees sway, writing,
emailing, arguing, letting go,
preparing for the morrow (much
preparing and letting go). Somewhere
the light moves in its measure west.
I rise and slip my cold hips
next to my husband's heat.

SSH

Bittersweet

The bad taste of my imperfections
clings bitter in my mouth and lids,
flashes taunts in neon. Voices whine
and deride until I run to you and hear
peace. It comes, this peace as I remember
my inheritance, a deep and brilliant light
glows blue and white in the pond
whose surface settles as thoughts
stop throwing rocks
and like bored children
find happier pursuits.

SSH

Al-Qahhar: the Subduer

Sometimes the blood runs hot in my veins,
way above 98.6,
way above rational.
I can feel it pound in my neck,
ring in my ears,
and my eyes become hard,
fixed,
chin jutting, sides of mouth pulled down.

And if I am lucky,
somewhere inside me
I hear this little laugh,
like the sound of a fountain in
a desert courtyard.
"Come to the shade," it seems to say,
and then I catch,
only in shadow, obliquely,
the twinkle in that
larger
eye.

KBN

Mystic

The woman asked the priest, *what is a mystic?*
Is it o.k. to call myself a mystic? I sat up to hear
for I am a mystic-wannabe, dreaming how mysticism
might take over my kitchen, spill its salt in the cupboard,
delicious and preserving. He answered that a mystic
is the one who is fully present, the one who sits,
fully sitting, who attends to eating with gratitude.

He used to call himself a mystic, but that was a stage of
development. Now, he does not grasp at titles. I think
of the joke where a man wins an award for humility
but in accepting, is disqualified, the prize taken back. I like
his answer but know a part of me crawls on the old stage,
the slippery one like a small ice-berg tilting where I stand
shouting, "I. am. a. mystic!"

And though life bobs in artic seas, and I, stiff
and numb, do not despair for I have sited the promised land.
Awareness warms me but does not transform. I seek control
urging, "Tides move me there! Toward that shore hazy with
folks dancing in ecstasy." I am disappointed when I learn
they celebrate the lavish and simple gift of the *moment*.

Tired of ineffective attempts to direct, I decide it's time
to give up the weight of a title; even good ones are ballasts
that balance in one season, list in another.

SSH

214

Transforming Presence

Actually, it was absence,
no internet for a while today;
mice evidently like
the taste of rubber,
makes them feel sophisticated
or something.

But I wrote without Facebook or Twitter or mail,
I wrote without Amazon or goodreads or...
channeling Dr. Seuss,
that's how it's been--
my mind playing along
in real-time,
choosing to see the humor of it all
but not missing the real rest.

KBN

Relationship

*When two people relate to each other
authentically and humanly,
God is the electricity that surges between them.*

Martin Buber

Root of Union

On an A-frame display they hang,
mugs of every shape and texture—
funny,
tasteful,
sip-able advertisements,
hand-glazed perfections,
full spectrum of colors,
some bold, thick and heavy,
one light china, the handle so small
even two fingers have to cuddle to hold it tight.

The old fashion coffee machine
moans while it heats up,
a language augmented with scent
prepping the audience
before the sermon.

Of course, the people gathering
will each hear a different message today,
screened through experience and chemistry
and the occasional faulty hearing aid.

But these cups,
these cups,
they will open their wide throats and
drink the liquid adrenalin
of communion--
many mugs
same fragrance.

There is a truth here,
steaming.

KBN

The Guest

All the appropriate masks sit
elbow to elbow,
passing the wine,
the bits of sweetmeat,
their laughter,
echoing out into the street beyond.
Strangers pass there,
or glance in,
wistful,
pale shadows,
these less socially-correct
bits of the self.

But all must be
invited in
otherwise, in our fragmentation,
we leave out beyond the door
unheard,
the most important Guest
and master.

KBN

A Good Host

The woodland grasses bend
to the wild sun spinning
in daisy spokes among galaxies
of dandelions. My steps scratch
percussive on the pebbled path.
My spine grows in the green welcome
of the upright firs, whose tips
comb the manes of homeless mists
that marble the pool of blue above.

Beauty travels these logging roads
and hosts us all. Even feces shine,
slug-glazed and the road gate,
discarded on its side, green twirling
round orange poles. There is something
tender about it all - purposed
but resting, askew and open.

SSH

Carrier of Memories

Dove soap.
One sniff, and I am back
amidst fresh flowers from her garden,
the way she wore her apron,
tucked up tight beneath her breasts.
How she would scrub the garden dirt
beneath her nails
furiously, with a little brush,
and occasionally a little bubble
would break away and hover over the sink, twinkling.
She kept chocolate in the high cupboard
and painted mountains in acrylic
while watching Days of Our Lives.
Even her leaving was a little slippery,
a heart growing silent
on the way to Indianapolis,
so she wouldn't cause
much of a bother to anyone.

KBN

Mother of the Weary

She lays the knitting down,
open-armed and fireside,
snow falling in rippling waves beyond the glass,
and I climb up
the huge distance into her lap--
already vaguely thankful
that hugs get filed somewhere safe
in the vastness of myself.

KBN

Absence and Return

Blue breaks through a twilight sky
between dark and bright rimmed puffs;
color travels to dark and I dream of morning,
yellow – enough rain and separation.

Far from me, your color comes in patches,
the miles and days hold you distant as the moon.
There you feed the chicks and bring your light
but brief - absence returns and dims the room.

Now home, I sit in my dream of a yellow morn
in quiet kitchen after a soft evening in a white bed.
In this light, I admire the tan coffee in thick mugs
and humming birds bowing suspended to sip nectar.

You make pancakes and bacon after a night of love.

SSH

Alchemical

In the new heat I worked,
fire again in limbs too still for too long,
drawing up light with the in-breath,
grounded and steady as I breathed out,
my eyes watching the rain
but gesturing warmth,
transformation,
awareness,
the energies of creation.
We must blaze,
our actions alchemical,
our thoughts,
seedlings lifting sunward,
our lives,
hearth-fires,
one to another.

KBN

A Marriage Blessing

May your feet warm your lover's toes
may your jokes be funny in old age
may you be hungry for whatever is for dinner
may you marvel at how your beloved sees God
may you glimpse how God sees your beloved
may you be the beacon of light when the seas are dark
may you be the sliver of moon that glows the night's clouds
in the home of your joined hearts.

SSH

Gentlest of Ways

The outpouring of our self,
with smile and extended hand,
with shoulders lowered from our ears,
and the listening eye, steady
draws the Other into our orbit.
We have yielded the walls
of role, title, age and gender,
become a space that the rigid heart
flows into,
effortlessly.
And effortlessly
transcends the duality of the meeting
and being met.

KBN

My Anam Cara

This friend helps me synthesize,
and grow the truth: *life is my size.*

Together we trust
and strengthen our eyes.

SSH

Granite

He carried you, tucked
in one dirty pocket--
over five acres of riding lawnmower chewed grass;
winding through
forest paths with blackberry vines
reaching for fabric with thorned hands,
weeding neat rows of the garden defined with
stacks of old newspapers,
resting on sittin' logs that sometimes held
rabbits,
or in the shade of the ancient oak,
registered officially
in the country's historical books.

He showed me once, how a dirty thumb
(fingernail blacked that day,
his usually clean chemist hands
remembering a farm boy childhood)
could sit right in the little depression
smoothing and soothing
summer sweat into granite.
Earth, solid and real,
pointing to the slower processes
of the broader life.

KBN

The Gardener

He hoes, plants, cuts, prunes, piles,
hauls, and digs for work and at home
for he loves the garden- its zebra grass,
geraniums, lilac, hydrangea, fuscias,
cedars, fig, camellias, dogwood, fir
and wild cranberry.

For her part, she loves the earth and air
that sweeps in with him, his shoulders
and back covered in tree dust and mulch.
She admires the patterns he mows in the lawn,
the elegant gate to yellows, reds, blues,
pinks and purples that glory in their keep
and color, but this is not enough for him;

he wants her to feel the hard, soft soil,
wonder at the seed, wait for the wisp
of sprout, pride in the height of the bean,
stalking round the pole, curl the tendrils
of her attention on the peas *she* planted.
To this end, he builds raised beds of timber,
piles them full with hens' manure, hoes it fine
and asks her to plant the summer garden.

She accepts, finds herself marveling at speckles
of seeds, muses as she pokes peas and corn into
the ground, pours carrot flecks into soft soil rows.

She knows she takes credit for many things,
mostly given and smiles when she hears him
call the vegetable garden *hers*.

SSH

Drifting Mist

I lied
on the way home to Seattle.
I told a woman traveling from New Orleans that
it never rains in the PNW,
just mists the skin—
what need for an umbrella?

And of course,
the God who loves to play,
sent winds to bend the fir trees low,
and enough rain to create
very fashionable mud-baths
licked with the drowning tips of spring grass.

We probably won't keep our electricity today.

Of course, I can also hear the birds sing
their voices
woven through the rain,
drifting spring tidings on the breath
when the rest of nature decides
to get a little more
dynamic.

KBN

Ahmed – Prince of Peace

Before you, boy, I knew so little.
I met a Palestinian once in an airport.
He guessed I was afraid and I was.
Newspapers print black and white words
like *all*, and *terror*, and *revenge*.
I've learned a little since then
of Naomi's poetry,
of Shaheen's music,
of the warmth of chickpea soup,
and the white of goat yogurt.

The soldier said he mistook you
for a militant – you, a 12 year old boy.
Ahmed, he was partly right. When you died,
militant spirits poured out of you
rampaging the hospital corridors-
demanding the lurking spirits of death
let live the Arab, the Jew, and the Druse
who received your lungs, your liver,
your heart.

What did you whisper to your father
that gave him the courage to love
the children who received these
while you, his own son, lie dying?
What kind of heart beats like yours,
miraculous heart, heart of Christ,
of every true prophet?

When the doctors lifted the still pumping heart
from your small body
true religion fell on its knees
begging to witness the crown of ages
lowered on your sweet head.

Ahmed, my prince of peace,
the next Palestinian I meet
will make me think of you
and I will want to kiss their feet.

SSH

Silent Sentinel of My Soul

They did not know,
as I laughed and taught,
argued and pushed them,
drank tea and ate spring rolls,
folded my legs on my straight-back chair,
leaning, fingers dancing with the rhythm of my words,
part of me was leaning back against You,
legs outstretched and ankles crossed,
watching them, so full of light,
they almost blinded me,
but you had my back,
my spine feeling your deep roots,
the smell of cedar reminding me
I but light a small fire as I teach,
and someday, all will drift as smoke.

KBN

Miracle Worker,

a name that brings to mind Annie Sullivan,
Helen Keller's teacher, who signed in her palm,

throwing her a life-line in her drowning isolation,
and pulling her aboard the lucky human race.

God tickles my palm when I hold a baby's hands,
laugh with a sick friend, purr in young spring sun.

I call such moments *miracles* when the light reveals
the lines of our belonging and our giftedness.

SSH

The Guardian of My Deepest Self

Who guards? And against what?

How much saner the world might be,
if we opened to each other,
put palm to palm
Namaste,
and took the time to look
past the eye's pupil
to the consciousness beneath.

If we stared, heart open,
(as well as our mouths, in awe)
and saw we are both mirror
and mirrored.

Infinity breathing even in the blinks.

KBN

My Portrait

She draws my portrait, intrigued that I can be
a daughter, sister, mother, grandmother,
all in one person. In her drawing, I float
under the rainbow's arc with fairy wings,
doubled and bright. With no hands or feet,
I hover as solid green and pink above the grass.
While I cannot stand or hold anything, my eyes,
large and open, see much over a slight curve,
hinting a smile. I can only mumble what I know
or want, but life suggests humor. My hair, long
and exotic, swoops in one line over my head
as it tangles in the colors of the rainbow.
I see how she draws from her ancient origin,
reveals our existence of mysterious oneness.

SSH

Inheritance

My elderly mother wants to see her childhood farm,
so we roll over hills of orchards and corn fields in search
of what turns out to be gone. I wake the next day
weighted under sadness of lost childhoods.

I slip through the sliding door to our hotel room.
Mother snores as I see in the clear air, an image
of a big mama, much bigger than my own. She reaches,
picks me up with a throaty laugh, folds me in round arms,
hugs me to her chest, then twirls me to sit on her lap.
My bare knees bend over her thighs and my chin raises
to laugh about something. We become a chorus. She laughs,
tickled by the joke I can't remember.

I peek back in the dark room to see if mom is awake,
warm at the sight of her, grateful for children and mothers,
this sweet bunch I've inherited andwho live in my skin.

SSH

Prophetic Voice

The whole object of the prophets and the sages
was to declare that a limit is set
to human reason where it must halt.

Maimonides

Lamb of God

I am not a salvational Christian;
I have seen lambs leap in the field,
their uncut tails flagging like cotton streamers,
their coat so white, before the rain
and mud and brushing up against life
crusts and splits that living Velcro.

They do not yield;
not when crowding up under the ewe,
not when butting each other,
rearing with tiny black bi-hooves raking
the cool air.

And when they do come to ground at last,
look how neat the bundle of legs
nose tucked in,
trusting the ground,
the touch of others,
and the fair sprinkle of stars
edging the field
before the moonrise.

The nobility of the lamb is in the life lived,
the waking and sleeping,
the eating and communion,
the fair and brilliant flash of movement
alive for life's sake,
present, aware and real.

That is the very lamb's play of God.

KBN

I Don't Care

I don't care if you pray to Jesus,
sit in meditation before Quan-Yin,
dance a wild spinning ecstasy around
the still center of your Sheik.

I don't care if you wear a pentacle
or hold up the latest scientific journal,
keep every kosher law
or run naked in dirty and crowded streets.

I don't care if you wave a fan over a sacred book,
bow five times a day to Mecca
show up to sing every Wednesday with the choir,
or chant from the Lotus Sutra.

Show me that you have something that,
when everything is taken from you,
when everyone has left you,
when even the sun pales and the oceans run
black and sickly,
the food is gone and the body stringy as rope,
drawing that last, terrible perfect breath,
you will still be able to say,
Yes.

KBN

Desire
Do you want us to fast? Logion 6 Gospel of Thomas

Yeshua answered,
stop lying and doing what you hate.
I hear, *be honest and do you what you love.*
How then does religion bind us with ropes
of suppression when in fact the Divine
leads us to risk and yes – terror, brandishing
the sharp knife of freedom? He asks
the hardest question: *what do you want?*

SSH

The Sword

Perhaps
you would not expect to lift the katana
and find peace in endless katas,
the light playing along the live blade,
the intricate knot-work folding the eye,
snaking in and out of shadows.
Or stare into the face of Manjushri,
ready to cut away illusion
with a flaming sword
and a sweet smile of all things.
Could you sight along the arrow
with Arjuna,
your gaze perfectly one-pointed
even when facing your grandfather,
your weapons master,
your half-brother?
Liberation, as Jesus said,
is not always best couched in the metaphor
of sweetness and being nice —
He Himself told others that he came with
a sword.
and Fire.

KBN

The Mirror Lies

The mirror lies, my friend —
you see one face, but already you are two,
the seer and the seen,
face to face.
You can't confront the inside by always looking outward.
And if you could peel back that furrowed brow,
no frame could hold your many reflections then.
Maybe better to simply shut your eyes and hear them,
the should-look-likes
the opinions,
the expectations
swirling
and
where did they all arise?
You threw open all the windows and door in your house, and
they flooded in.
At first, they promised to remodel and repaint,
fix the squeaks
re-carpet the living-room,
but you let them move in
not happily, perhaps,
but still, you fed them.
Sit here quietly beside Me a moment.
Let Me be your mirror, just for these few breaths,
and tell you,
there is a still small voice under all that hubbub.
Can you heed it?...

With this single, standing reflection
you can simply recall
being
one?

KBN

The Ride

Bound for glory, this train
drives a wild route.
You need nerve
round this locomotive.

Not now you say?
Press your ear to the track
and hear that it is near,
hear the hum running
through ancient stories,
rumbling with Presence.

Ah, now the whistle pines
in the air. Its longing opens us.

You fall in terror at the blur
and the roar. It is the response
of the living, and now it's time:
get up and see that you
are already on the ride
of your life.

SSH

Rant

Sometimes, it's not useful to know too much;
all scripture, in all traditions,
are only man speaking to man,
the woman's voice hushed whispers,
echoing them
and sometimes,
not even that.

I listened to a modern Sufi talk about chivalry,
and he illustrated the ideal with the story of his aunt,
killed in the resistance against Germany.
He held her up because she didn't give up
anything when tortured.
She died not for religion or country
but for freedom.

I've never met freedom, how about you?
Touched its hair, kissed its eyelids?

Just one more incident of sati, really,
another female body on a man's fire.
All gone, her stories, her music, her love of children —
these were things that could have healed people,
no matter who won the war.
The Pir held her journal,
but he was not really celebrating her life.

There will always be violence.

Look at our sun
the raging compression and wild explosions
as matter shares space with matter.
The Pir's aunt would have always had a bonfire to throw
herself on;
its always there, for any of us,
even if we playfully change its name over and over.
It's always a waste
to be barbequed for ideology.
I distrust anyone who makes it a virtue.

I admit it; every time I think I have found a lover's path,
a patented "Way" to God so that I might have
the company of other lovers,
it's tainted by history or culture.
Ramakrishna and Kabir both had no trouble
with a wife throwing herself on her husband's death pyre.
How can the rest of their words make up for that kind
of blind horror?

Even Rumi, locked away with Shams,
how did his wife feel then?
We know how his sons took it—they killed the interloper
and we?
We are shocked.
But why?

I will tell you the truth:
any worship of another human or their personal ideas
is idolatry.

And the Buddha and Jesus we have inherited?
aloof, a-sexual, noble martyrs in the end,
well,
I want to put a shuttle in their hands,
let them throw it back and forth,
let them weave something with *all* the colors of life.
If they can do that mindfully, lovingly,
and then fall into bed and lose themselves
in the embrace of warm, living reality?

Those would be men I could learn from.

This is not how the Mystery made us,
to stand up and out and be made into statues
with fingers that have become so swollen as they
point to the moon,
that the fullest, brightest light
can't seep through,
that our hands become so rigid
they can't curve around another's flesh
and feel the fragile bones beneath.

Even the women's ways, the new ones —
they are a kind of lie as well,
burying menstrual rags in the yard,
painting bodies in wild creative rushes,
changing the language to reflect equality, equity--
wake up!
Can't you just take your child's hand,
walk with him along the beach and see
the ever present interplay of male and female,

hear the roar of the ocean,
calling that one note
that requires all of our voices to chime
and then
slice the apple,
pat the dog's head
and call it benediction enough?

Would you douse the raging fire and
stop groveling before these idols we keep making for
ourselves?

Can you surrender discipline in exchange
for a more gentle touch,
a more liquid response,
rather that one flavored with mission, with martyrdom,
or tinged with high ideals of
global change or political statements?

Because that?

That will take a strength,
a will,
a million times stronger than climbing onto a cross
or the wearing ochre cloth
or memorizing political rhetoric —
living the full life God has granted you
is much harder, my friend,
than following any time-muddied path
because it wants all of you.

Thy Will be Done but
without any filters or props
and when you are through,
can you nurse the living energy you must pass on
with your very crumbling bones set as paving stones,
and let that be
enough?

KBN

Holy Spirit

Tradition speaks
of the Holy Spirit,
the third person
in trinity, that mystery
which entered
into Mary's belly
as sperm to her egg,
dividing cells
that grew into Jesus,
that fire of flames on men's heads
making many languages one,
wind rushing on Pentecost
inspiring preachers to wear red,
and place reader-board letters
to advertise their sermon titles,
"Come Spirit Come"

Losing tradition, I speak
of the Holy Spirit, as that
which fills, embraces, lifts,
compresses, heals, wounds,
is me and you, connects all.

I admit a rascally fantasy
of sneaking to the church lot,
prying open the reader board,
and change the title to, "Holy Spirit,
Bring Us to Our Senses"

I would hope the preacher would dance,
shout, "Hallelujah! People! You can see,
taste, hear, smell, and touch God, as we
swim here, in the ocean of the Holy Spirit!"

SSH

Yes!

There was, in the silence
between
the words,
such an eagerly anxious waiting
to relax and find.
Those who never find, never experience trouble.
Those who never experience trouble,
never know how it is to reign,
one leg in meditation, one foot on the ground,
ready to push off;
one hand gesturing up and away,
the other, bearing witness to the seed's knowing.
Resting always teeters on the edge of stagnation,
instead of the effortless putting off of masks,
comfortable at last in skins broader than the universe,
brilliant as the flame in the center of the heart.

How do you teach without uttering a word?
How do you bow without something to bow to?
How do you convey history without
missing
one
moment?...

Those are the koans we should be dancing, drumming,
sitting, painting, gardening and sipping tea with
until
we forget
what
questions
are for.
Until,
there is only
Yes.

KBN

God the Liberator

The interior's critic forges the bars. A foundry
of voices shape a molten message of lack
that cools to hard habits of seeing the self,
incomplete. Apologies abound,
stretching the length of the prison wall.

Probation began when you snuck in and asked me
to put my ear to the cell floor. I heard humming;
first note of creation, you said. You showed infinity
in the blue, framed by the jail window. You lifted
me through the bars to travel with clouds, tiny birds
along horizons. Then you put my eyes in yours.
At each guard, we gazed, cupping their fragile light
to shield it. We breathed them brighter.

After that night, the guards and I conspired
to break out, work for better pay, and move
to a better neighborhood.

SSH

Necessary Being

Necessary is a thorny crown:
a word of boundaries,
shoulds,
neediness;
a warlord's word,
the sword of the dualist.

It's not like you can ever
fall out of God,
as a friend is fond of saying.

What we need, what is really necessary,
(say, with a quirking smile)
Is simply this:
Thy will be done.
And done, evermore,
as it
spills sweet water over the land
so the contended well is forever
unnecessary.

KBN

Have Ears that Hear

It is not enough to just read the words,
not enough to just move through the world,
listening to only the surface of things.
We are called to be diggers,
unearthers,
reanimators,
creators.
And for that,
we must listen in ways
that strip and narrow and flay
as well as
broaden, deepen and expand.
We must, like God,
hear it all,
without purposeful plugs,
without hands pressed over
the delicate ridges of our ears.
Would you be brave and compassionate,
the seed planter and the harvester?
Then you must have ears
that
hear.

KBN

Pardoner

I quite enjoy deliverance,
forgiveness if you will,
from this image of a squished
and little god, needing
lots of apologies
I endlessly supplied.

Now I study your example
as lessons on the art
of offering kin, friends,
church, work-mates,
strangers, enemies,
and myself indulgence,
absolution, allowance,
release, mercy
and kindness.

Thank you for this mentoring,
Master Pardoner. You,
who need pardon nothing,
but for our sakes,

pardon all.

SSH

The One Who Weeps

I sat for a time,
holding
the new Mr. Spock and the old.
I was in love you know,
only a kid, but my!
Those pointy ears
and that perfect logic.
He felt safe and sane,
distant and pure.
When emotion bled through,
I always knew it was real and
sourced deep.
And of course, it didn't hurt that
Spock was stronger than humans;
could pinch a neck and save
the whole cosmos.
But in the 2000-something remake,
Spock is a child of his rage,
the outer exterior, the lidded pot;
his heart, open and available;
so his logic is not enough of
a gatekeeper to hold his passion in.

Interesting that
today
we reinterpret the character of Spock, once
full of seeming control
the one who bent science to his will,
who stood alone, heroic

now angry, needing others:
father, lover, friends.
Fragile.
The scientist who weeps.

KBN

Always the Same

The question is always the same,
Though it takes many forms.

Can you say YES?
It's that easy.

It's that hard.

KBN

Lord, Hear My Prayer

There are things I could pray for:
freedom from self-guessing,
from imposing an image over my
own sense of who I am.
If I get started, I suppose,
the list could grow
endlessly.

I'll spare you that.

Instead, I would ask
for one simple thing:
dispel my ignorance.
Hold up the mirror
kept in the most secret space,
that I might see You
looking back at Yourself,
laughing.

KBN

Trust

*You may not know where you're going,
but you know that so long as you spread your wings,
the winds will carry you.*

C. JoyBell C.

A Meditation in Flight

Eleven turkey vultures float close
to tops of trees lining the near field.
Their great wings spread in praise
of hunger my heart knows. These
scavengers darken the world below
like bombers casting shadows gliding
over rooftops and steeples, rumbling
the questions of old religion:
what is living and what is dead?
Hunger, a truth serum smells
the carcass of lies that proclaim,
I am not afraid to die.
They inspire me, these birds,
to open my palms and let scatter
pieces of life, bloodied with fear
What does it matter what eats
the carcass left behind?

SSH

Born

Teresa: though you be feisty,
a favored mystic, heroine, example,
and mentor of mine, your prose
disappoint me. You call complexities,
vipers, belittle the journey, distance me.
I close your book and hear inspiration
call me to your poetry.

And there, there your words
twine fingers into mine,
pull me running to a living God,
who questions, confesses, entertains,
pleads with us to enjoy, laugh, receive,
love it all, be ocean, hold swimmers.

Teresa, you rock me snug singing
in the nursery a lullaby of my birth,
fruit of your marriage to the divine.

SSH

Bind Me Back

Bind me back to a time,
when religion was not
another word for psychology;
when the shaman's journey
or the Christmas Mass
told the story of relationship,
illuminated the ties that bound
life to life to
Mystery.

We work too hard now–
what does my life mean?
How does the past haunt today?
Who are all these voices clamoring inside?
I wonder —
why not invite it all in and serve tea?
And afterwards, gently,
walk the line between earth and water and sky,
hum a hymn from childhood,
and recall
not one of us arose from independent nothingness.
Reweave yourself, but intuitively,
in the meal served,
in the hat knitted and passed on,
in the laughter at the grocery check-out line.
If sin is simply all that is "unripe",
then explode with flavor, with juice,
or if it is time,
with a fearless releasing to earth.

Live interwoven with it all,
and tell me
where then can you really fall?

KBN

Necessarily Here

I started to write of God
as a Necessary Being*s*,
and saw how accidentally,
I added a final /s/,
but at seeing it this way,
I left it. My fingers knew
the truth:

to speak of God
as *necessary*
is strange - as if
we could speak
of Reality as needed
or *un*. Better to look
in the mirror and see
that we are here,
necessarily and needed.

So much poetry in verbs
and nouns of *ing:*
wing and fly dancing,
fling and sing floating;
working, grieving, crying
belong to the goodness
we can taste when we value
the necessity of our being.

SSH

Needing Poison

In sun and rain, our lives hang, fruit swelling

sweet round a hard pit, hidden in our depth.
We understand little why Divine Mystery,
placed in our hearts, seed, pointed like hands,
praying, yet coated with cyanide.
Do you know inside the apple's tiny seed
and peach's rutted pits poison coats tender
white generations of the morrow? Infants
of creation come with guardians round their core.

What if the bitterness of lust, murder, greed,
fear, in thin-layered portion protect eternity?
What if wisdom holds us to the sun's heat
to sugar the waters of our life? Ripe, we drop,
trusting darkness belongs to the mystery
at our core. Something quiet and ferocious
guards the seasons so we harvest our fruit.

SSH

Holy Mother

I do not picture
Mary sniveling in a corner,
hand over her mouth
in a classic Virginal state.

No, I prefer to see her standing
considering,
head tipped a little to the side,
her arms loose, so her heart
can be wide open
even before an angel.

Her "Yes"
is also mine.

KBN

Gentlest of Ways

The first time I tried to swim
at age five in the frigid water
of Discovery Bay, I despaired,
of the sea's bitter cold,
the hardness of rocks,
teaching me my sinking nature.

I learned close to my mother,
who rested, legs splayed sitting
in a pool of blue and warm water.

There, I leaned back,
raised my eyes,
spread my arms,
and felt myself float,
learning in shallow depths
a lesson, gentle and generous,
how to trust my buoyancy.

SSH

God of Salvation

Ancients needed salvation
in the heat of not hell but battles
going badly. Those of us not ancient
or in battle receive our first deliverance
when our mothers welcome us.

Perhaps my second birthing
and time of salvation came
when God urged me to shake
my- fifteen year- old fist at the Ogre
others called Divine, the one who
mostly damned, offered salvation
to the perfect. I never was.

At fifty, salvation comes in eyes
that enjoy the way God sees cliffs,
dropping into the blue inlet,
comes in hair blowing in the wind
wildest mid-sound on the ferry's bow,
in skin tingling cheeks in chill air,
and ears that hear the gulls watching.

Salvation comes through senses,
enjoying the gospel that fear
would hide from us.

SSH

The True Rest

I've heard the words —
established in thee,
Be still and know that I am God,
on and on such sayings go,
but
I like the idea that
true rest must come
after
we
are
speechless.

KBN

Joy

What for all humans is inevitable? Joy!

The Mahabharata

Getting to a Place Called Marvel

The temple train drives a wild route.
You need nerve to witness, let alone
travel this trip. Press your ear to the track.
Do you hear it humming? Do you feel
its heat? It runs a path of ancient lovers,
singing and burning with Presence.

Ah, the whistle blows - its longing
heats us. The blur and roar of mystery
nears, no matter our staggering terror.

The mystery is - you are now on board,
careening full and fast through your days.

Never mind *how* you got on. Open you eyes.
Wake up and marvel that you travel through
a green wilderness on the tracks of your life.

SSH

Resurrections

Green tea with jasmine
dark chocolate wrapping an almond
the leaf of a tree, so new and wrinkled
rows of yarn, waiting to be touched
small muzzle in my cupped hand
the pool's blue sigh as I slip in,
giggles from the kitchen,
my mother's patient silence:
resurrections need not be
the stuff of epics.

KBN

A Patch of Gray

Tree tips wreathed in fog
and the ferry calls and calls,
People huddle monk-like,
staring through the windows
at blown glass and soy candles,
the puddles at their feet edged with oil rainbows.

Look up into this patch of gray sky!

I lit a stick of incense today,
the smoke rolling over the cold black wood stove,
edged around a picture of crow, a frog, a salmon and a bear,
and I wondered
if they enjoyed shaking off silver droplets of water
into cooler air
as much as I.

KBN

Rainmaker

I've hidden my drum,
tucked the flute away,
and sit now,
beneath my cedar.
The sun flicks its branches with red
and St. Francis is growing moss.
We have no need of rain here;
at last, the long winter's clouds
are pressed to the horizon line
like a frill on the blue skirt of the sky,
and I
echoing with that sometimes-manic rush
of spring,
tamp it all down for a bit,
and let myself grow
warm and green.

KBN

Master of Harmony

The bees do business on a Sedum-Wall-Street,
touch and lift, bee-banking for honey money,
pollen portfolios swing by their knees which

makes me long for human business
that would hum with their harmony.

SSH

Vine

I will braid Thee into my hair,
roots and all,
and in the autumn,
let the riot of grapes brush my ears,
hang like tresses, purple and red,
until my blood runs with wine,
and my gray eyes green up,
so that all I see shimmers with Your
bountiful, inebriated giggles.

KBN

The Light - A Saturday Gone Right

This day weighs heavy in a world
grey with marine air, anchored to stay.
A forecast without sun, of muffled sounds,
dim colors adds weight to this sad season
of summer leaving.

We wander lackluster wondering how
to entertain pre-school grandchildren.
My husband doesn't want to push the kids
on city swings, so he marshals us to pack
the truck aiming for a mountain road, past
Lords Lake, the reservoir. We catch hints
of each others' smiles as he drives a little
too fast, shimmying over washboard ruts.
He swerves into a gravel pit after siting
a water fall, which we aim to see up close,

but the path narrows, steepens, pebbles roll,
our feet slide. I call for grandpa to grab Broden,
the two-year-old as I direct Raeya, then four to clutch
exposed roots. Grandpa, the outdoorsman, stamps
a foot-hold while gripping Broden's wrist. The boy,
unconcerned, dangles, fills his free hand with pebbles,
throws them as he twirls.

The dog climbs handily above us then slides grinning
as dogs do, skids her chest into the boy, and then seized
by adoration or shame in her ill-timed game of Red Rover,
she begins licking the boy who bats her away.

We begin to laugh at it all including the folly of our plan,
decide to forego our destination. We crouch sliding each
with bent knees around a child until we reach the edge
of the stream, then peel off our shoes and socks to stand
quiet in the water as we listen to its creek-song, rising
into air, shimmering and clear to the blue above the fog,
trapped in the valley below.

SSH

Awakener

I face east to write
and today,
the sunshine exposed
the intricate and eddying whirls
of gray and white steam
twisting millisecond hurricanes
that dissipated
with my breath,
grew lacey,
spacey,
as the green tea cooled.

Such bounty before
the
first
sip.

KBN

Optometrist of the Heart

Confused, I see myself in a sepia tenement,
musty and faded

habits lie on stains of discontent
on rusty springs

then I breathe the truth of color as you meant-
inhaling freshness.

SSH

Forgiver

They say you are divine because you pardon,
but why not *For* and *give* to mean
giving before-asked, like placing a spring
before a desert traveler thirsty and dry,
saying *yes* before hearing *please*?

Am I not blind to insist that you
have anything to pardon?
How many times must I kick
and trip on the gospel of Jesus
as I fail to see the good news:
to be human is enough.

Why do I lay face down in the dirt
after falling over that corner-stone
as all the while I long to stand
on the ground called,
I am enough.

Let me forgive myself, You, and all
that fills my lap with anything
but the warm body of this infant,
whose name means Delight.

SSH

Playmate

"Yah! Let's! Come on!
Yahoo! I LOVE this.
Hah! How Fun!
Wheeee-Hoo!
Jump! Again!!! Woa!
Look! I'm a shape!!!!
Hold my hand!
Let's do it together!
Again! Please – this
is fun!
Don't Stop, Grammy!"

Before I release to sleep,
I pray, *Thank you
for playing with me today.*

SSH

The Vine

He tied the tender stem to the fence where
leaves spread green by the old wisteria.
It wraps its old woody stem round the rail.
In season soon we'll smell the summer rising
over blossoms yawning perfumed mouths
next to the young stars of purple clematis.
It rouses from heel to head hallelujah notes,
weaving in this paradise like ribbon in the twist.

SSH

About the Authors

Sue Sutherland-Hanson used her Masters of Teaching in a career teaching English to international and immigrant students at community college. In midlife, she earned her Masters of Divinity from Earlham, a Quaker seminary, emphasizing writing as ministry. Sue grew up in a commercial fishing family in the Pacific Northwest, where she lives with her husband and extended family.

Kimberly Beyer-Nelson holds a master's degree in comparative religion and a certificate in holistic healthcare from Western Michigan University. For over twenty years she has taught Hatha Yoga, Qigong and meditation. An internationally published poet, essayist, novelist and artist, she lives with her son and husband on Bainbridge Island in the Pacific Northwest. You can visit her blog at http://guhacaveoftheheart.blogspot.com/

Made in the USA
Charleston, SC
05 December 2014